Department Store Disease

Department Store Disease

James Bryant

McClelland and Stewart

© 1977 by McClelland and Stewart Limited
ALL RIGHTS RESERVED

ISBN: 0-7710-1720-0

The Canadian Publishers
McClelland and Stewart Limited
25 Hollinger Road, Toronto M4B 3G2

Printed and bound in Canada

Canadian Cataloguing in Publication Data

Bryant, James, 1908-
  Department store disease

ISBN 0-7710-1720-0

1. Department stores – Canada. 2. Department
stores – United States. 3. Department stores –
Canada – Anecdotes, facetiae, satire, etc.
I. Title.

HF5465.C32B79   658.8'71'0971   C77-001139-X

Dedicated to my wife, Bea, who helped me keep the disease at bay throughout my career, and to my daughter, Bev, for twenty-one years the joy of my life.

My thanks to Ruth Carlysle, Debbie Burn, Lynne Dunsmuir and Bob Jamieson, of Toronto; Jack King, Grimsby, Ontario; Barbara Bell Matuszewski, Sewall's Point, Florida; and the many, many friends and associates who helped me with suggestions and facts.

Contents

Foreword

Everyone knows how to run a department store, or thinks he does. Perhaps this is because most people go into stores every day to buy items they wear, use, eat, or admire. Some merely browse, for the department store has also become a medium of entertainment. These same people are less inclined to become armchair executives of other businesses, such as banks and insurance companies which they visit less frequently, or factories, with which they rarely have anything to do.

The department store, however, is among the most complex of enterprises. To operate one successfully, expertise is required not only in merchandising, but in finance, transportation, manufacturing, real estate, architecture, engineering, demography, and computers. Moreover, for optimum results, the department-store executive must co-ordinate the activities of experts in these fields with skill and care.

In the United States and Canada, many department stores founded in the latter half of the nineteenth century have grown into institutions of such importance that they are as famous as their home cities. In his book, *Minding the Store*, Stanley Marcus intimates that for some years Neiman-Marcus has been nearly as well known as Dallas itself. Such a store takes on a personality and, to many of its customers, assumes human characteristics. Consequently, victims of merchandising and service errors can become as emotionally entangled with stores as with people. Have you ever noticed that the patient customer, who waits calmly in line for a very slow bank teller to process his deposit, can deteriorate into a raving monster when instant service is not forthcoming from the department store down the street?

Because the emotions of so many people are aroused by their rela-

9

tionships with department stores, I reason that they will be interested in factual accounts of happenings in, and amusing anecdotes about, these stores. As television and movie producers, from time to time, intrigue audiences with fictional tales about department stores, surely their curiosity can be whetted by true stories that are often stranger than fiction.

I was there when things happened, and I was privileged to be associated intimately, over a period of more than forty years, with some of Canada's most renowned merchants. Among them are A. J. Gilbert and Norman Douglas of the Hudson's Bay Company; the incomparable C. L. Burton and his two talented sons, Edgar and Allan; S. S. Fletcher, and Charlie Stewart, all of Simpsons.

Still another distinguished merchant gave me my first job, in a stock room of the Hudson's Bay Company. His name, somewhat prophetically, was Robert Simpson, but he was no relation to the noted founder of Simpsons, the company with which I spent most of my career.

After three years of working for Robert Simpson, I was forced to consult a doctor. He subjected me to almost every test then known to medical man and told me that he knew what was wrong but could not help me.

"Like so many of my patients who work in department stores," he said, "you are afflicted with 'department store disease.' I cannot do a thing for you, but you can do something for yourself. If you are able to find a way to control the pressures that build up in your business, instead of letting others – like your superiors, those reporting to you, and customers – control them, you might survive. Otherwise all you can look forward to are stomach ulcers."

Apparently, this malady is a by-product of the department-store profession. No less a merchant than Rowland Macy who, in 1858, founded Macy's at 14th Street and Sixth Avenue, New York (later, at its present location, 34th and Broadway, the world's largest store under one roof), died in 1877 at the age of fifty-four – reportedly from stomach ulcers.

Now, some forty years after seeing that doctor, as I look back and decide to share my experiences, I recall the recent comment of a friend: "Jim does not have ulcers, but he is a carrier." I was fortunate in that I retired with good health – and an appropriate title for this book: *Department Store Disease*.

J. B.
January 1977

Introduction

Except for the automotive and communications industries, the department store has influenced the lives of North Americans more than any other business. Yet, no institution is as much taken for granted.

The department store seems always to have been there: to older generations, on the same corner downtown; to younger people, in the same shopping centre. In the United States, the first stores to become departmentalized were founded within fifty years of the Revolutionary War. In Canada, they were born and grew up concurrently with the nation itself. Morgan's preceded Canada's 1867 birthday by a few years; Eaton's and Simpsons were founded shortly after.

Even though most Canadians and Americans are interested, often intrigued, with the activities of the department store, they seem less than curious about its history and development. Familiarity brought about by continuous contact is likely responsible for this.

But since people are interested in other people, not things, such as stores, a reminder that retailing is a business where the human factor is and always has been dominant might help stimulate curiosity. Each store was started by a person, usually a very interesting person and, no matter how efficient computers and other machines become, the best retail organizations are always directed by thinking men and women, able to translate their knowledge of consumers' needs and wants (there is a difference), even dreams, into items on store shelves. The superior thinkers are always the superior retailers.

For these reasons, beginning this book with a short account of how the department store came to be what it is today, particularly on this continent and even more particularly in Canada, seems appropriate.

Prostitution may be the oldest profession in the world, but retailing – that is, the sale of merchandise to ultimate consumers – is said to be the oldest business. This claim may bother some dedicated merchants who, like me, consider the practice of retailing to be a profession, but we are reluctant to compete with prostitution for what would be the rather dubious honour of ranking first.

It is a fact, however, that primitive peoples conducted retail businesses based on the bartering of food and weapons. Later, these earliest merchants were replaced by traders and peddlers. By 3000 BC individual shops or booths were common, and by the eighteenth century small stores carrying only one line of merchandise – forerunners of modern specialty shops – had become the principal method of retailing.

During all this time, the department store could be said to have been waiting in the wings for its cue to come on stage. But that could not happen until about the middle of the nineteenth century, when economic and social forces unleashed by the industrial revolution had developed to the point that the department store could become a viable business enterprise. Before that time, numerous attempts to operate stores carrying many types of merchandise had foundered. But the growing migration of the rural populace into cities, brought about by the burgeoning of factory towns, the development of public transportation, and the advent of electricity for elevators and lighting, made the modern department store possible.

During the nineteenth century many towns and cities with populations of fifty thousand and more sprung up, and horse-drawn buses (later electric-powered street cars) enabled the inhabitants of these communities to travel conveniently to city centres. A number of imaginative merchants, for the most part operating small dry goods stores, envisaged the opportunities on the retail horizon. Almost simultaneously, in France, in the United States, and in England, these men assembled many different lines of merchandise under one roof.

Department store historians* generally seem to agree that the first store with different lines of merchandise (men's wear, women's

---

* Among the first to write about department stores was Emile Zola, the French novelist. About 1880 he wrote, "The strength of the department store is increased tenfold by the accumulation of merchandise of different sorts, which all support each other and push each other forward."

wear, housewares, etc.) set up in physically separated areas of one building, was Bon Marché in Paris.

This renowned department store was started in 1852 by a merchant named Aristide Boucicaut. But stores very similar to Boucicaut's were being opened about the same time in London and New York. And, since all of these stores began as specialty shops, adding departments as circumstances and the initiative of the owners permitted, it becomes difficult to decide where and when the modern department store did, in fact, get started.

Before becoming a department store, Bon Marché specialized in fabrics by the yard, or piece goods, as this line of merchandise was called for many years. But Shoolbred's, the first store in London to develop into a department store, began around 1817 with dry goods, a rather vague category of merchandise that was more extensive than piece goods, but excluded hardware, housewares, and groceries.

In New York, Alexander Turney Stewart opened a small dry goods store on Lower Broadway in 1823, and he gets my vote for having started the whole thing. Perhaps I favour Stewart, an Irishman from Lisburn near Belfast, because I think of the department store as a North-American phenomenon and am reluctant to give credit to France or England. And, the fact is, Stewart expanded his business three times before Bon Marché opened its doors. By 1848, four years prior to Bon Marché's advent, Stewart had moved into his huge and famous Marble Dry-Goods Palace on Broadway at Chambers Street. This building, which still stands and still looks like a department store, occupies a full block on Broadway and a two-hundred-foot frontage on City Hall Park. The Dry-Goods Palace carried on a wholesale business in combination with the retail store until 1862, when the retail departments were moved into a new six-storey building, known as the Cast Iron Palace. Within a few years, this establishment covered the entire block between Ninth and Tenth Streets, and between Broadway and Fourth Avenue. This is the structure which most North-American department stores later used as a model. The iron columns supporting each floor permitted customers a view of vast areas of the store, uninterrupted by walls.

Confirmation of my selection of Mr. Stewart has come from a most unexpected source. Gore Vidal, in his novel *1876,* has one of the principal characters, the Princess d'Agrigente, visiting New York for the first time, enquire of her escort the name of the owner of a huge palace at Fifth Avenue and 34th Street, which overshadowed the Astor homes nearby. The escort replies that a Mr. Stewart, a merchant, resides there. "Not *the* Mr. Stewart of the department store?" asks the Princess. "The same. But, of course, no one knows him. No ones goes to his house." "But *I* know him! Or I think I met him at his marvelous department store."

It is then explained that "department store" was a new phrase used to describe "a huge emporium in which many different things are sold, with each kind relegated to its own section or department, an innovation apparently of Mr. Stewart."

The Princess was thirty-five years old in December of 1875 when she was shown Mr. Stewart's house. That would make her twelve years old when Bon Marché opened in 1852. It seems most unlikely that a young woman who was to become a princess could spend twenty-three years in Paris between 1852 and 1875 without being aware that Bon Marché was departmentalized. (My only reason to challenge Vidal's intensive research for his book is that he refers to Stewart as being Scottish rather than Irish!)

Stewart died, childless, in 1876, and twenty years later the business was taken over by John Wanamaker of Philadelphia, whose success in that city had made possible the opening of a branch store in the larger New York market.

The evolution which enabled some specialty stores to become department stores involved more than simply locating different merchandise lines in physically separated areas. Radical new retailing policies and practices, almost as vital to the development of the department store as the basic principle of housing all departments under one roof, were being adopted at the same time by the same men who had decided that the future of retailing would focus on the department store.

Although there may be some question as to whether Boucicaut of Bon Marché originated the department store concept, there is little doubt that he pioneered new retailing principles. His novel policies inspired others, notably Wanamaker in Philadelphia, and Timothy Eaton and Robert Simpson in Toronto, to do likewise. His innovations were quite revolutionary!

Prices of all items in stock were plainly marked on merchandise and were the same for all customers. The practice of haggling over prices, in vogue up to that time, was abandoned.

Customers who found merchandise unsatisfactory were permitted to return it for exchange or for refund.

The practice of taking high mark-ups, resulting in low turnover, gave way to using low mark-ups to provide a competitive advantage over other stores while increasing sales volume, turnover, and, ultimately, profits.

For the first time customers were permitted to inspect merchandise without feeling obligated to purchase. Prior to the arrival of the department store, each visitor to a specialty store was expected to make a purchase. An uncomfortable atmosphere developed when a transaction was not completed. This important and welcomed change in shopping custom was, perhaps, as much an outgrowth of the department store itself as a planned policy of store owners. Browsing naturally developed when people walked through departments where purchases were not anticipated to those that were their targets. Whether this practice was adopted by design or by accident, it became one of the most important factors in the evolution of the department store. People developed an entirely new attitude toward shopping: for the first time they were in a position to conveniently compare quality and prices offered by all the stores on a particular product. Department stores, as a result of this economic force, located as near each other as possible in city core areas, and the good ones prospered side by side. They became the magnet that brought the people downtown.

Except to the most fastidious of department-store historians, it is of small significance whether the modern department store began with Bon Marché, Les Grands Magasins du Louvre, and au Printemps in Paris; Shoolbred's, Whiteley's, and Harrods in London; or Stewart's, Lord & Taylor, and Macy's in New York. Origins notwithstanding, the development of the department store into its present social and economic entity has been largely a North American phenomenon. And, although the United States – with a greater number of densely populated cities – had a head start of some twenty years on Canada, Canada has produced some of the truly great stores of the world.

The Department Store in Canada

Although Benjamin Bowring (great-great grandfather of P. Derrick Bowring, present head of Bowring's department stores and distinctive gift shops) opened a small store in Newfoundland in 1811, credit for the first retail establishment in Canada to achieve true department store status must go to Henry Morgan. In partnership with one David Smith, he opened a small dry goods shop on Notre Dame Street in Montreal in 1845, when the population of that city was less than fifty thousand. By 1860, after Smith had left and Henry's brother James had joined the firm, it had moved to larger quarters on McGill Street. In 1866, three years prior to the opening of Eaton's and six years ahead of Simpsons, Morgan's relocated again, this time in a new, four-storey structure on St. James Street at Victoria Square, which was departmentalized and employed a staff of about one hundred.

Also in 1866, James Ogilvy went into business with a tiny shop on Mountain Street near the old St. Antoine Market in Montreal. Nazaire Dupuis, first of the Dupuis brothers, followed in 1868 with a small fashion store on St. Catherine Street. However, a few years would pass before these stores would qualify as department stores.

But it was in Toronto that the Canadian version of the department store enjoyed its most spectacular growth. The two men who founded the stores which were to dominate the marketplace for more than a century had strikingly parallel careers. The similarities began in 1834, the year in which both founders were born.

Robert Simpson, a Scotsman from Morayshire, and Timothy Eaton, an Irishman from Ballymena, were apprenticed to merchants near their places of birth. Simpson served in a grocery store, Eaton in dry goods.

Both emigrated to Canada as young men in their twenties, and both started their careers there as store owners in small towns outside Toronto – Simpson in Newmarket, Eaton in St. Marys.

But small towns could not support their ambitions, so both moved on to the greater challenges and opportunities offered by Toronto. Once there, however, both entered into short-lived partnerships: Simpson with his cousin James, and Eaton with a man named Allison.

Then each, after less than a year of partnership, made a historic move to the west side of Yonge Street: Eaton, in 1869, to the site just south of Queen Street now occupied by Simpsons; and Simpson, in 1872, to just north of Queen where Eaton's downtown store now stands. Toronto's population had nearly doubled in the decade between 1870 and 1880, and the two stores had prospered accordingly, requiring larger quarters to accommodate a growing sales volume. Eaton and Simpson took advantage of sites that could be rented or purchased on Yonge Street, north and south of Queen; and by 1883 the stores had switched original locations, and settled downtown on the sites that are the nuclei of those occupied today.

Both men maintained very personal interests in their customers and meticulously adhered to policies which were to be the bases of future growth of the two companies. Eaton died ten years after Simpson, in 1907, but their successors continued to expand the downtown properties. And expansions persist to this day. With the building of the Simpson Tower in 1968, Simpsons completed its expansion into the full block between Yonge and Bay, and Queen and Richmond. Eaton's is countering with a gigantic project, the Eaton Centre, which eventually will cover most of the ground between Dundas and Queen, and Bay and Yonge. Eaton's new store in the centre will be at Dundas and Yonge, so for the first time in more than a century the two stores will be separated by a greater distance than the width of Queen Street.

For more than one hundred years, the two stores flourished and grew along Yonge and west toward Bay, on Queen. In the process, a competitive situation was created that is unmatched in the annals of department store history. Even the giant stores of New York, the legendary adversaries Macy's and Gimbels, have not generated such competitive fervour. The battle for the lion's share of Toronto's vast retail market raged without interruption across Queen Street until the 1960s, when it began to spread to the suburbs. Even there, hand-to-hand duelling, perfected by a century of conditioning, has been favoured over long-range fighting. Wherever possible, Eaton's and Simpsons have become close neighbours in suburban shopping centres, often as associates or partners in the ownership of the centre. (This phenomenon is more fully discussed in "The Developers.")

Both Simpsons and Eaton's have had their ups and downs in those hundred years. (Except for the depression in the thirties, Eaton's course was almost all upward until 1951.) But, the competition between the two companies, which gradually spread across Canada, has provided the stimulus for growth that has enabled them to dominate Canada's department store industry since Confederation.

Eaton's

Eaton's small dry goods store opened in Toronto in 1869. Sales were slow at first, but when, after a few months of operation, Eaton adopted a policy of "goods satisfactory or money refunded," business took a permanent turn for the better.

His other policies were probably inspired by Boucicaut of Bon Marché: all merchandise was sold at clearly marked, fixed prices; and he sold for cash, a policy which his successors were forced to abandon in 1926 as the twentieth-century charge account concept evolved and became vital to department store operations.

About 1874, Eaton's mail order business was started with a distribution of handbills in Toronto. Ten years later, their first catalogue appeared. It has been said that, with the possible exception of the Bible, Eaton's catalogue had a greater effect on the lives of the rural population in Canada in the fifty years after its introduction than any other book. It is quite safe to say that families who lived on farms in the West during this period would not dispute this assessment.

Timothy's eldest son died as a young man in 1900, and Timothy died in 1907. By that time, John Craig Eaton, another son, had taken over the business. In 1905, Eaton's Winnipeg store and mail order operation were opened. Goodwin's was acquired in 1925 as a Montreal base. An outlet was opened in Hamilton in 1927, in Saskatoon and Halifax in 1928, and in Calgary in 1929. Acquisition of some twenty small stores in Ontario, in such places as Ottawa and Kitchener, added to the network. In 1948, Eaton's reached the west coast, when the eight stores of David Spencer were acquired, and the highly regarded Vancouver store provided a suitable flagship for Eaton's operations in British Columbia. By 1950, Eaton's had permeated nearly every city, town, and hamlet in Canada with stores, branch stores, and more than three hundred order offices in smaller centres.

The story of Eaton's is embellished in a later chapter of this book, but no history of that company – no matter how capsulized – can omit reference to its white elephant, the College Street store.

Eaton's planned and built this facility in the late twenties. At that time, Eaton's management was sure that by moving into a new and beautiful building at College and Yonge, Toronto's centre of retail activity would shift from Queen and Yonge to the new location. Apparently, Eaton's people wanted to hedge their bets, however, for they offered to sell Simpsons the block across from the proposed new store on Yonge Street, on the condition that Simpsons would move with them. As C. L. Burton wrote in his autobiography, *A Sense of Urgency*, "The devil they knew was evidently to be preferred to the devil they didn't know."

Simpsons wisely declined the invitation, but Eaton's went ahead with the project. The new store was opened as the depression began in 1930, about as unfortunate an opening year as could have been chosen. And, although the facility was new, handsome, and possibly as well stocked with home furnishings as any store in North America, it is believed to have been Eaton's big loser for many years. At this writing, there is talk about it being razed to be replaced by an office building complex.

Despite their problems with College Street, Eaton's was the undisputed leader in Canadian retailing for the country's first hundred years. Its decline from the number one position is examined in "The Competitors."

While Simpsons (through its own efforts and through Simpsons-Sears) and Eaton's were destined to dominate the department store industry in Canada, other stores, particularly the Hudson's Bay Company and Woodward's in the West, made important contributions to the growth and development of department store retailing in Canada. Moreover, many others that did not branch out became important institutions in their home towns: Ayre's in St. Johns;

Wood Brothers in Halifax; Manchester, Robertson, Allison in Saint John; Paquet in Quebec City; Ogilvy's in Ottawa; Robinson's in Hamilton; Smith's in Windsor; Goudies in Kitchener; Smallman and Ingram's in London; William's in Regina; Spencer's in Vancouver. Many have since been absorbed by larger companies; regrettably, some have closed.

Before providing some background on Simpsons, on which most of the material in this book is based, a word about the Hudson's Bay Company and Woodward's is needed to complete the Canadian department store picture.

Hudson's Bay Company

Almost every Canadian school child has been taught that the Hudson's Bay Company was granted a charter on May 2, 1670, by King Charles II of England, to trade in furs in the Hudson Bay regions of Canada. Thus, "The Bay" is the oldest of all the retail companies in the world.

Its entry into the department store field was an outgrowth of fur-trading outposts which were established in western and northern Canada to trade with Indians and Inuit. Some of these posts developed into stores as forts became villages and as the Canadian Pacific Railway spread across western Canada spawning cities and towns.

The Winnipeg store started in 1881. The Calgary store dates from 1884, Vancouver from 1887, and Edmonton from 1890. Only Victoria deviated from the pattern of following railway development; it began in 1859 during the period when the company administered Vancouver Island as a colony for the British Government and was supplied by sea.

The Bay's invasion of the eastern Canadian department store market began with the acquisition of Henry Morgan and Company of Montreal in 1960. At that time, Morgan's had four branches in Montreal, two in Toronto, one in Hamilton, and one in Ottawa. The takeover gave The Bay an ideal launching pad for future penetration of the coveted eastern market.

An unusual event which took place in 1969 may well have had significant effects on the Hudson's Bay Company and all other department stores in Canada. In that year R. J. Butler had been appointed president of Eaton's, and Donald McGiverin left that company to become The Bay's managing director of retail stores. In 1972 he became president and chief executive officer of The Bay.

This shift was unusual because, unlike in the US, senior executives of Canadian department stores rarely change their allegiance. The move is also significant because, since Mr. McGiverin's arrival, The Bay has acquired the A. J. Frieman Company with five stores in Ottawa, and an interest in the well-established G. W. Robinson Company of Hamilton. It has also opened several new stores, including the sixty-million-dollar Toronto flagship store at Bloor and Yonge.

The Bay's attack on eastern markets seems to have gained so much new momentum that more will be said about it in "The Competitors."

Woodward's

Before moving west, Charles Woodward had successfully operated a number of stores in Ontario. With his first Vancouver store, opened in 1892, he founded a great North American department store organization, as well as an important department store family. Spurred on by Vancouver's rapid population increase and the gold rush in the Klondike, for which the city became the principal supply centre, the store (located at what is now the corner of Main and Georgia), was an instantaneous success.

By 1904 larger quarters were required. A move was made to a new site, which became the nucleus of the present huge store at Hastings and Abbott Streets. It began as a three-storey structure, and was enlarged many times between 1904 and 1947.

Woodward's first branch store opened in Edmonton in 1926. In the 1950s branches began operations in shopping centres in New Westminster, Victoria, and West Edmonton. Stores in South Calgary and South Vancouver followed. Today twenty-one stores are doing business in fifteen cities.

Woodward's has been one of the innovators in the department store industry. A drug department was opened in 1896, long before most North American stores realized that this lucrative business could be shared with the corner pharmacy.

22

In 1919, Woodward's introduced a self-service system in the food departments, to combat the inflation that followed World War I. This may well have been the very first "groceteria." In any event, it was remarkably successful, expanding continuously until it became the world's largest food operation under one roof. Perhaps more important, it enabled the store to retain this traffic-generating department during the 1940s, when most North American department stores were abdicating the food business to the fast-growing supermarket chains. To this day, food operations contribute substantially to the company's fortunes.

The foresight of Woodward's management was demonstrated once again in 1930, when it correctly foresaw that adequate car parking facilities would be vital to the survival of the downtown department store. In that year, with another department store first, Woodward's connected a large garage and parking lot to the Vancouver store by an underground passage. And innovations continue. To combat 1975 inflated rents in London, England, Woodward's has moved its buying offices in that city onto a renovated river barge, which floats on the Thames River near the Houses of Parliament.

Charles Woodward died in 1937, but he left four sons to carry on. His eldest son, John, was responsible for much of the early expansion. P. A. Woodward was the food marketing genius; the Honourable Colonel W. C. Woodward, president of the company during the thirties, forties, and fifties, was honoured for his outstanding contributions to the city of Vancouver, to Canada during World War II, and to British Columbia, by being made Lieutenant Governor of that province in 1941. His son, C. N. Woodward, carries on today.

Simpsons

This sketch of the background of department stores in Canada must be rounded out with a brief account of Simpsons' history and growth.

Not only is most of this book based on my career with Simpsons, but Simpsons, together with its partly owned subsidiary Simpsons-Sears, is now the largest department store complex in Canada.

As has been noted earlier, Robert Simpson and his arch rival, Timothy Eaton, had curiously parallel careers. It is interesting to contemplate what may have happened to the department store business in Canada had not Simpson died in 1897 at the relatively young age of sixty-three. For, while Eaton was more rigid in his adherance to the policies that made his company great, Simpson was the more imaginative merchant. Moreover, Simpson fought back from reverses – including two disastrous fires – that would have ended the business careers of most men, perhaps even a Timothy Eaton. At Simpson's death, his store was much more impressive than that of his rival across Queen Street. His six-storey building had been completed in 1896. It was a skyscraper in Toronto at that time, and had replaced a similar structure occupied in December 1894 that burned to the ground three months later.

The new building contained thirty-five departments in open, airy settings, and a fine restaurant. It was equipped with the latest elevators, lighting fixtures, a cash railway system, and the best telephone switchboard of any comparable store in the world. So, in 1897, with business booming in a splendid new edifice, with the mail-order business rapidly expanding, Robert Simpson was matching Timothy Eaton stride for stride. But his death that year ended the rivalry.

From this point the two companies developed along rather different corporate lines. Unlike Eaton, Simpson had no sons and only one daughter, who had no interest in carrying on the business. The Simpson company was sold to a group of Toronto men led by H. H. Fudger, a wholesaler. Joseph W. Flavelle, an industrialist, and A. E. Ames, a financier, were the other investors. Under Fudger, expansion of the Yonge and Queen property continued and, in 1905, Simpsons began to spread to other Canadian cities, when the John Murphy store in Montreal was purchased.

In 1912, a new era at Simpsons was born when Fudger transferred C. L. Burton, the managing director of Fudger's wholesale business, to Simpsons as assistant general manager. Charles Luther Burton was destined to create a dynasty that would have made Robert Simpson proud indeed. From the moment in 1912 when he moved to Simpsons, Burton became a key figure in the company's development. His sons and grandsons carry on direction of the company to this day.

By 1920, with business flourishing in the stores, and mail-order activities growing (mail-order expansion had included new buildings in Toronto, Regina, and Halifax), Sir Joseph* obtained financial control of the company by purchasing some of the holdings of the other two original partners. While Flavelle took a more active interest in the business, Fudger and Burton continued to manage day-to-day operations.

In 1925 the present holding company, Simpsons, Limited, was formed by a public issue of common stock, and in 1929 Flavelle sold his controlling interest in the business. Burton, along with J. H. Gundy, founder of the Wood-Gundy investment house, and D. H. Gibson, general manager of Simpsons mail-order operations, outbid two American groups to obtain control. Burton was named president and his old friend and mentor, Fudger, chairman.

C. L.'s son Edgar joined the company in 1925, and his son Allan, now chairman and chief executive officer, ten years later.

Like most Canadian enterprises, Simpsons went through difficult times during the depression years in the thirties but C. L. Burton was endowed with ample measures of ingenuity and determination with which to meet the challenges of those first years of the company under his control. That he was equal to the task is demonstrated by company records of the period which show that, while large and small businesses were failing every day, the victims of declining sales, Simpsons, although suffering sales setbacks along with the others, lost money in only one year, 1932. In addition, it is a mark of the man that Burton vowed not to increase the number of unemployed by reducing the staff in relation to the decrease in business. To be sure, salaries and wages were lowered in keeping with the times, but no employee was released.

After World War II, C. L.'s sons, Edgar and Allan, returned from wartime duties to help in the business. Edgar had been retail administrator for the Wartime Prices and Trade Board, and Allan had served overseas with the Governor General's Horse Guards from 1940 to 1945.

The Burtons have always been dedicated to keeping store facilities up to scratch. Even in the depression year of 1937, air-conditioning of the Toronto store was undertaken. Mail-order facilities in Toronto, Regina, and Halifax were improved in 1941 and, in 1944,

* J. W. Flavelle was knighted for his World War I service as chairman of the Imperial Munitions Board of Canada.

25

the Smallman and Ingram store in London, Ontario, was acquired. In 1946, the purchase of R. H. Williams Company gave Simpsons a large department store in downtown Regina to complement the mail-order operation on the city's outskirts.

Edgar Burton, who had succeeded his father as president in 1948, engineered the most important development in Simpsons history, the formation of Simpsons-Sears, now the largest department store mail-order company in Canada. As so often happens, events leading up to that important corporate decision began by accident rather than by design. A chance introduction to a Sears executive by the son of a friend, who had taken a position with that company in Brazil, started Edgar along the path that was to end in Simpsons and Sears joining forces in Canada. The executive arranged to have Edgar meet General Robert E. Wood, chairman of Sears, Roebuck and Co., in the summer of 1951. The first informal meeting was followed by the discussions, studies, and negotiations that resulted in the new company beginning operations in January 1953.

The deal was not complicated; in fact, when compared to some corporate mergers – say, those engineered through Paul Desmarais' Power Corporation – it was child-like in its simplicity. Yet, to this day, if the questions I am asked are to be taken at face value, many prominent businessmen – even financiers and stockbrokers handling transactions in the shares of Simpsons and Simpsons-Sears – fail to understand it. Simpsons simply turned over to the new company the mail-order business which consisted of 4 control stores, 322 order offices, and 64 agencies. Sears put up $20,000,000 in cash, calculated to be the value of these Simpsons facilities. Simpsons retained its five department stores in Toronto, Montreal, London, Halifax and Regina.

Thus, while Simpsons and Sears became equal partners in Simpsons-Sears, Sears had no financial interest whatsoever in Simpsons. In fact, the agreement provided that Sears would not purchase Simpsons' stock on the open market. The investor who buys shares in Simpsons, therefore, acquires at the same time an interest in Simpsons-Sears. If he buys only Simpsons-Sears shares, however, he does not participate in Simpsons' fortunes, good or bad.

If Simpsons and Sears are equal partners in Simpsons-Sears, one may wonder where the shares being traded on the Toronto and Montreal stock exchanges come from. The answer is that, at incorporation, three classes of shares were authorized: 600,000 class A, 2,000,000 class B, and 2,000,000 class C. Classes B and C are voting shares and were issued to Simpsons and Sears, Roebuck respectively for their $20,000,000 investments. The class A shares were sold to employees of Simpsons-Sears and Simpsons on a stock-option basis, and to the Profit Sharing Retirement Funds of the two companies. Class A, non-voting shares first appeared on the market as holders retired or died and liquidation became desirable. Simpsons and Simpsons-Sears continue as equal partners through equal ownership of the voting stock. Originally Simpsons and Sears each held approximately 43.5% of the outstanding shares. As new class A shares were issued the percentage of ownership of each party by 1975 had declined slightly to 41.3%.

A condition of the agreement which has confused investors, customers, and even employees is that Simpsons agreed not to open stores beyond a twenty-five mile radius of their existing stores in Toronto, Montreal, London, Halifax, and Regina. In return, Simpsons-Sears agreed not to encroach on the twenty-five mile limit in these areas, but to concentrate their efforts in all other parts of Canada. In 1972 the agreement was modified to provide that any area of Canada could be served by a Simpsons or Simpsons-Sears store or by both if the two companies mutually agreed it was desirable. This made possible the entry of Simpsons-Sears into the lucrative Toronto and Montreal markets.

The magnitude of Edgar Burton's 1951 decision to enter into the agreement with Sears is highlighted in Simpsons, Limited annual report for 1975. It shows that while Simpsons had more than tripled its investment in Simpsons-Sears to $64,350,800, it received cash dividends of $43,929,000 with further earnings of $79,297,000 yet to be distributed by Simpsons-Sears – a grand total in earnings from the investment of $123,226,000. Simpsons shareholders' equity has increased by more than $212,000,000 in the 22 years of Simpsons-Sears operations. Simpsons sales, which were less than $100,000,000 in 1952, amounted to $547,939,763 in 1975.

Simpsons-Sears sales in 1975 were $1,548,600,000. If Simpsons-Sears had not been created, it is fair to assume that half of these sales would have gone to Simpsons, which would have retained the mail-order business. If this had been the case, Simpsons' sales would have about equalled Eatons' estimated sales for 1975 of $1,400,000,000.

Allan Burton, who had been appointed president in 1964, became chairman of the board and president in 1968, when Edgar Burton died. Allan has been the imaginative guiding force at Simpsons throughout the period of its most spectacular growth. In the past decade, sales have increased by more than 120%, and eleven new stores have been added to the chain. In 1970, Charles B. Stewart was named president when Allan became chairman and chief executive officer. Charlie was the first non-Burton to occupy the presidential office since 1929. In June, 1976, he became deputy chairman of the board and Edgar's son, E. G. (Ted) Burton, a Simpsons vice-president for some years, became president. Allan's son Jamie, a general merchandise manager for the Ontario region, is presumably in training to help continue the dynasty begun by his grandfather.

* * *

I should not want it to seem from the foregoing corporate and statistical information that department stores are impersonal institutions, run by absentee owners and shadowy executives in remote offices. On the contrary, the department store is an institution in which the human factor is dominant, where people are much more important in the success or failure of the enterprise than are buildings and fixtures, and where relationships between employees and customers and between fellow employees produce every human reaction from love to loathing.

Until the 1960s, when a proliferation of suburban branches and evening hours resulted in split shifts and inconsistent supervision, the department store in North America very much resembled a community, a town or city where everyone knew what everyone else was doing. Its executives were like a community's powerful leaders – the wealthy mill owner, the largest employer, the mayor, the chief of police – who exercised some control over the lives of citizens. Both towns and stores have their petty thieves and major con artists; store "characters," like those in a town, provided humour; and rumour-mongers kept their tongues wagging, repeating and inventing stories of clandestine love affairs and scandals.

In fact, the department store provided a village-like atmosphere and, like a village, incorporated every strength and weakness of the human character. The store buildings merely represented the town's boundaries. This community syndrome had its roots in the paternalistic, almost feudal, approach that was characteristic of many of the very first department stores. Many employees of those stores actually lived and ate on the premises.

In 1890, Whiteley's, the historic and once-huge London department store, housed and fed 2,000 of its 5,500 employees. They slept in homes that took up almost an entire street, and ate in dining rooms in the store building.

Around 1860, a Chicago store provided this set of rules for its employees:

> The store must be open 6 a.m. to 9 p.m. the year round. The store must be swept; counters, shelves and showcases dusted; lamps trimmed, filled and chimneys cleaned; pens made; doors and windows opened; a pail of water, also a bucket of coal brought in before breakfast (if there is time to do so); and attend to customers who call. The store must not be opened on the Sabbath unless necessary, and then only for a few minutes. The employee who is in the habit of smoking Spanish cigars, being shaved at the barber's, going to dances and other places of amusement, will surely give his employer reason to be suspicious of his integrity and honesty. Each employee must pay not less than $5.00 per year to the church, and must attend Sunday School regularly. Men employees are given one evening a week for courting and two if they go to prayer meeting. After 14 hours of work in the store, the leisure time should be spent in reading.*

One department store historian**tells of morning prayers and bible readings before opening stores for the day's business. He suggests that the practice died out about the time of the introduction of the cash register. If the suggestion implies that the replacement of the open till by the cash register reduced stealing more reliably than praying, it is one which could be questioned.

For me, the similarity between the department store and a small town is very real indeed. Banff, in the Rockies, where I grew up, was even like The Bay in management. Being a national park, it had no locally elected government. The park superintendent, like Hudson's

---

* John William Ferry, *A History of the Department Store*, New York 1960, pp. 24-25

** Ferry, P. 27.

Bay Company managers, was subject to absentee control. He was a puppet and his superiors in Ottawa pulled the strings.

And, just as department store morale goes up and down with every rumour, promotion or high-ranking executive shift (not to mention whether or not the air-conditioning is working properly), so the spirits of a small town thrive on great happenings, be they earth-shattering events, local catastrophes or celebrations, or scandal – real or imagined.

An unceasing series of rumours kept the gossips busy in Banff, and Grace Metalius would have found our resort town as suitable a setting for *Peyton Place* as the New Hampshire tourist town that she did use. Everyone knew what everyone else was doing – or thought he did.

One reason for this was that, other than during the tourist season, when only the occasional store-keeper – or leashed dog – was tied to his place of business, every mobile person in Banff attended all important events – such as fires.

If a fire occurred at night, there were no exceptions. When the Prince of Wales, later King Edward VIII made his first visit to Canada shortly after World War I, Sir James Lougheed (then Minister of the Interior in Robert Borden's conservative government and grandfather of Peter Lougheed, the present premier of Alberta), was Canada's official host in Banff. This was an ideal arrangement since Lougheed's ministry controlled national parks and the Lougheed family of Calgary had then (and still has) a large home near the Banff Springs Hotel.

In preparation for hosting the prince in royal fashion, Sir James had had delivered to a railway siding in Banff a magnificent maroon-coloured Marmon automobile. Private cars were still a rarity in Banff at the time, and about as many people attended the unloading of the huge machine from a flat car as greeted the prince some days later. For a time, the car was the principal attraction on the streets of Banff. In the early morning hours a day or two prior to the prince's scheduled arrival, however, the fire bells began to toll. As was the custom, all residents of the town, children and adults, jumped from their beds, hastily dressed and proceeded to the fire. I vividly remember being, at age eleven, in the vanguard of the multitude crossing the Bow River bridge in the direction of the Banff Springs Hotel.

At the Lougheed home a large crowd had gathered and was awaiting the arrival of Banff's usually efficient fire department. A garage behind the house was being consumed by flames. Fanned by a brisk breeze, nearby spruces looked like Christmas trees decorated with lighted candles as sparks set their needles afire. And Lady Lougheed, Peter's grandmother, stormed up and down the long verandah of the house as if on the warpath, shouting, "God damn the fire brigade!"

The absence of the fire company is easily explained. At that time the department was changing from horse-drawn to motorized equipment. One of the teams of dappled greys had been replaced by a fire truck. Previously, at the first sound of the alarm, firemen slid down a pole, harnesses dropped on waiting horses, and the engine was away, accompanied by a fanfare of clanging bells and clattering hoofs.

On this one and only occasion the firemen placed too much faith in the new mechanized truck, for it would not start. By the time they had reverted to the horses, the Lougheed garage and the prince's transportation were a heap of ashes. Rumour had it that one of the Lougheed children, perhaps Peter's father, had left a cigarette burning in the car after a midnight spin.

*   *   *

In Banff, sex scandals usually involved men and women whose daily activities kept them in close physical proximity. The dentist with his nurse, and the young male high school teacher with his favourite female student (who requires after-class tutoring), were among the juicier stories. Similar situations in department stores had similar results. Male buying supervisors and their young female buyers, with whom they were required to take trips to the New York, Montreal and Toronto markets, were particularly vulnerable.

When I was merchandise manager of Simpsons Montreal, Hartley Lofft was general manager; Hartley told me that when he was a buyer of ladies' dresses in the Toronto store, he asked C. L. Burton for extra pay for making trips to the New York and Montreal markets. Mr. Burton encouraged male buying supervisors to have female helpers around when selecting women's fashions; the decrease in buying mistakes warranted the additional expense. Lofft had a most attractive assistant, and felt that he should receive danger pay for keeping his distance.

Some time ago, a US department store chain had a rash of problems with store managers getting mixed up with female employees. Most of these resulted in family relations so strained that they came to the attention of general management in Chicago. Some ended in divorce, and all caused management problems in the stores.

The number of cases was sufficient to cause concern at the highest executive levels. Why so many? Why all of a sudden? Why were all the women involved cashiers? Finally, why was the problem confined to a group of stores in the mid-west under the same regional management?

A personnel supervisor, sent out from Chicago, soon found the answers. All the stores in this particular district had pretty much the same layout. The cashiers operated in a protected room or cage, situated in the lowest level of the store. As a result of defalcations in some stores by cashiers, so the story goes, head office had dictated that store managers must go to the cash room at the end of the day and supervise the handling and bookkeeping of the days receipts. The system was soon found to be impractical, and rescinding instructions were issued. If received by the regional management of the group with the problem, they were never implemented. The male managers continued to supervise the female cashiers in rooms so small that it was impossible to avoid physical contact. Operation Cashier would begin after the store had closed and all other employees had gone home. As time went on, it took longer and longer to balance the cash.

*   *   *

As a youngster in Banff, I often knew more about the facts of a situation than all of the town's rumour experts put together. Between the ages of ten and fourteen, I was the CPR telegraph messenger. For a boy, it was quite the best job in town, although it did restrict my activities in sports and other youthful pursuits. In the summer, I was paid $45 a month, precisely my starting wage at The Bay after a university education! In the winter, working before and after school and during the lunch hour, I earned ten dollars less.

Perhaps I was being conditioned in Banff for a role in the department store business, for I learned to work like a dog, to be intensely competitive, and to develop my imaginative potential. I

32

also learned how to set work priorities and to get things done, and the priceless quality of confidentiality was imbued in me at an early age. The hours of a telegraph messenger were long and, although not physically tiring, thinking was important. (I quickly learned to obtain payment for collect telegrams before I handed them over, and to obtain a signature for a death message before allowing the recipient to read it. One fainting customer taught me that.)

As for imagination, much was required when a telegram recipient's address was simply, "Try Rooming Houses"; and I devised a fool-proof system to foil dogs that chased my bicycle: speed up, put on the brakes, start again, and run into the dog. Every dog so treated remained, in future, snarling on the front steps, and after a year or two on the job I rode the streets of Banff in relative freedom.

What could be better conditioning for a life in retailing, where so much depends upon doing many things simultaneously, than arranging a stack of a dozen telegrams, all of which have to be delivered during a lunch hour?

And finally, confidentiality. Before the long-distance telephone took over, all urgent out-of-town communications were carried over telegraph wires. I was, of course, sworn to secrecy, and I knew that my job depended on not mentioning a word of the contents of any message, even to my family. At times it was almost unbearable. How did I ever restrain myself from telling my friends that our twenty-year-old school principal, who had been Joe Cronin's teammate on a California college baseball team, had been offered a professional contract!

When the silent-screen star, Estelle Taylor, was making a movie in Banff, I lived on the passionate daily messages she exchanged with Jack Dempsey, who was then courting her. Keeping my oath of secrecy was easier in this situation because I was secretly in love with Estelle myself, and preferred to live in a dream world in which I didn't have to share her with anyone, even Jack Dempsey.

My love for Estelle was not merely the fanciful thoughts of a twelve-year-old for a pretty face on a movie screen, although she was quite the most beautiful creature I had ever laid eyes on. I saw her at close range two or three times a day and talked to her at least once. Our telegraph office was in the Mount Royal Hotel, located on Banff's principal downtown corner. The stars, supporting players, and camera crews stayed at the hotel and ate there. As Estelle moved about the hotel, I had many opportunities to arrange accidental meetings. More important, instead of delivering her telegrams to the desk clerk, I always waited until she passed through the lobby on her way to her room so I could exercise my prerogative of delivering the messages in person. In the course of obtaining her signature, I usually managed to exchange a few precious words.

Jack Dempsey wooed Estelle away from me, but my career as a telegraph messenger conditioned me not only to work hard, use my imagination, and be competitive, but to accept with some resignation the daily disappointments that go with life – and department stores.

The rivalry between Eaton's and Simpsons had nothing on my home town. Banff might well have been the most competitive town in all Canada. Everyone fought tenaciously for every tourist dollar in sight. About every house had rooms for tourists. Even wives of well-paid government officials rented such rooms.

When I was eighteen I went into the sight-seeing business to help pay for a university education. (The four-year course took eight, as money was only available every other year.) A seven-passenger touring car, which occasionally accommodated ten, was used for the purpose. I was classified as an independent, and as such my opportunities to attract business were somewhat restricted. Independents were permitted to solicit business only from a stand on Banff Avenue, where the cars lined up single file, and moved toward the front of the line in turn. We were also permitted to solicit business from a designated area at the CPR station. In the late twenties as many as twenty trains a day passed through Banff carrying hordes of tourists – mostly Americans. But little business came to the independents, because the famed Brewster brothers had a concession from the CPR which provided that their agents, and theirs alone, could solicit on the platform and in the station house. Independents were required to park across a highway some sixty yards from the platform, and holler at the top of their lungs to any tourist who escaped the clutches of the Brewster agents, as numerous at times as the tourists themselves.

My first visits to the CPR station were unproductive. As many as twenty independents would line up on the lot. Several of them had been driving sight-seeing vehicles since the days of the tallyho. And they knew the ropes. When tourists managed to elude the Brewsters, these men could somehow spot them from afar and run their cars up to the platform before I had time to start mine.

But after a few days I devised a fool-proof system whereby I got the first customer, and the old-timers had to take what was left. I was young and I could run. When a group of tourists responded to the frantic calls of the independents, I would run to the platform, select the smallest piece of luggage and, indicating that I would be right back, carry the bag to my car. Possession of the luggage made the customer a captive, and a new competitive system came into being over-night. All independents had to adapt to it. The order of business was in direct relationship to the speed at which the independent could run.

On one memorable occasion I sprinted across to the platform to pick up a small bag belonging to a delightful young couple who were returning to their home in California from a round-the-world honeymoon trip. When I returned with the car, two of my competitors, old fellows who had reluctantly adopted the new system, were wrestling with the suitcase of another customer who had eluded Brewster's agents. A tug-of-war had developed, with each driver tenaciously holding one handle of the bag. The bag's owner, correctly anticipating destruction of the handles, was simultaneously screaming and beating the two over the head with his umbrella. Eventually one handle gave way and another row developed over who would pay for the damage. As I drove my honeymooners towards the Banff Springs Hotel, I explained the background of the incident. They laughed all the way to the hotel and occasionally for days afterward, as I drove them through the Rockies. I laughed also, not only because the tug-of-war scene was incredibly funny, but because the new system – my system – was providing for me, at the expense of my competitors, a steady flow of customers like the young couple from California.

In the years to come I found that introducing new systems – systems that changed the rules of the competitive game for department stores – was the most challenging and rewarding of management responsibilities. If a competitor inaugurated a new merchandising, operating, or promotion technique, it became the challenge of the moment to cope with it, adapt to it, or perhaps outdo the other store at its own game. If the idea and the execution of it were your own, a period (usually short-lived) of smug self-satisfaction could be enjoyed.

35

The Impossibles

Murphy's Law: "If it is possible for the worst to happen, given time it surely will."

Bryant's Amendment: "The smaller the community or store the more time it may take."

Murphy's Law is always in force in the department store business. On any given day, few store executives, isolated in their management floor offices, would be surprised to learn that their most dreaded nightmare had become a reality – "they" had forgotten to open the store.

One morning in the late thirties, F. F. Martin, then general manager of all Hudson's Bay department stores, left his office on Main Street to stroll over to the big Bay store at the corner of Portage Avenue and Vaughan Street in time for the nine o'clock opening. The store covered a full block along Portage between Vaughan and The Mall, and the first door in Mr. Martin's path was the south Vaughan Street entrance. At 9:03 he found it locked. The centre Vaughan Street door proved locked also. Peering inside, he could see no indication that anyone was coming to his rescue.

In those depression days, customers were not usually clamouring to enter The Bay at 9 a.m., or any other time of day. But Mr. Martin believed that all doors should be opened on the stroke of nine as advertised, if for no other reason than to give him access. He marched double-time around the block trying every door en route. All were locked except the last one, on Portage Avenue, by which he was finally able to gain entrance. Mr. Martin was not amused.

But a merchant is supposed to have, without exception, two qualities: a sense of humour and eternal optimism. As Mr. Martin seemed to be lacking in both, I could not consider him to be much of a merchant.

This inherent tendency toward calamity makes it difficult for department stores to rectify problems because, once a situation goes haywire, it seems that every effort to put it right leads to a new disaster. There are thousands of disaster stories in complaint department files, but the ones that follow must be all-time classics.

When I was an assistant manager for the Hudson's Bay in Winnipeg, I lived with three other assistant managers. Our conversations were usually interesting, educational, and laced with humour because my housemates were exceptionally talented. They were Jack King, who later became the first Canadian vice-president for sales of Texaco Canada; Stan Smith, an engineer who now has his own successful business in Vancouver; and George Brown, a prince of a fellow who died at a young age before he had the opportunity to fulfill what certainly would have been a brilliant career.

At lunch, at a coffee shop across Vaughan Street from The Bay, the group was usually joined by Wally Landreth, another of The Bay's bright young men, now vice-chairman of Canada's Tariff Board. At these gatherings the morning activities were reviewed and decisions made as to how the company could best be run in the future.

One day Jack King did not turn up for lunch. When he failed to return to the apartment at his usual time in the evening we began to get concerned. Eventually he arrived tired, hungry and bedraggled. "What happened to me today should not have happened to the general manager of Eaton's," sighed Jack.

That morning before store opening, Jack, who was then research assistant to George Lawrence, the store's comptroller, was on an assignment which required him to cover the entire store. He began on the top floor, criss-crossed the floor and walked down a corner stairway to the floor below. On the landing of each floor was a washroom; men's and women's facilities were located on alternate floors. Deep in thought about the task of the moment, Jack miscounted the floors. Comfortably seated he was horrified to hear the sounds of female voices and high heels. He tucked his telltale legs up out of sight waiting to escape. But the opportunity never came. Each moment of silence was followed by new footsteps and new voices.

Eventually he decided that he was there for the day and made the best of it by enjoying conversations that few men are ever privileged to hear. The impossible material Jack gathered that day entertained us through many lunches and dinners.

One evening not long afterward, George Brown was in a rare sombre mood. Murphy's Law had reared its ugly head and George confessed that he was not likely to have his job in the housewares department by the next morning. He had made a mistake that is almost always disastrous in the department store business: he had taken something for granted.

Early that day, George had received a telephone call from G. H. Klein, general manager of the store, informing him that Mrs. X, a wealthy customer, had been trying in vain for some days to have an ordinary corn broom delivered. Furthermore, Mr. Klein had said, if a broom did not arrive at Mrs. X's home on the afternoon delivery, George could find a new job.

Although Mrs. X had received many items instead of a broom – including a whistling teakettle and a pot scrubber – the most curious item was yet to come.

George was taking no chances. He personally selected the broom. He made out the sales bill. He even phoned the manager of the delivery department to say that Mrs. X's broom would be on its way down the chute shortly and that it had better get to Mrs. X's place that afternoon. Otherwise, George said, what the store manager was going to do to him would be insignificant compared to what George would do to the delivery department manager.

As George brought the broom to the wrapping table, he was called away to the telephone. Before taking the call, however, he warned the wrapper not to touch the broom until he returned, for George intended, as a final precaution, to wrap the broom and place it in the delivery chute himself.

The telephone call proved to be a lengthy one and when George returned to the wrapping station, the broom and the sales bill were gone. Then, George made his critical error: he assumed that the broom had gone through the system in the normal way, and that it would be delivered to the customer. Blithely, George began adjusting another complaint.

Now if Mrs. X had received her broom, or even a new whistle for her kettle, there would be no story. But what was delivered to her that afternoon was more than the most paranoid store executive could have thought up.

The wrapper George had cautioned not to touch the broom took a coffee break while he was gone and the girl who replaced her was new on the job – so new, in fact, that Mrs. X's parcel was the first she had ever handled. The wrapper also knew nothing about the housewares department, so how could she be expected to tell a broom from a cash register handle?

And it *was* the handle of the cash register that was delivered to Mrs. X. To anyone not connected with the store , it seemed inexplicable that Mrs. X should receive a cash register handle in the afternoon delivery. But there was a mad logic behind it. The handle was used to operate the cash register only during emergencies when the electric power failed. At other times it often served as a paperweight to hold down sales bills. Whenever a broom, mop, or any long-handled implement was to be wrapped, the clerk did not place it lengthwise on the top of the wrapping desk where it could be cumbersome and difficult to match with its sales bill. Instead, the broom was propped against the desk with its business end on the floor. The sales bill was then placed on the desk, directly behind the broom, and the cash register handle or some other handy paperweight was used to anchor the bill.

For the new wrapper, who had been taught that the sales bill was always placed under the merchandise to be wrapped, it was a straightforward matter of wrapping. The wonder is that it had not happened before!

I heard later that Hudson's Bay management had changed the system – not because customers were winding up with cash register handles instead of brooms, but because there were never any cash register handles around during power failures.

* * *

Murphy's Law was working overtime in the spring of 1971. It all began in April when a friend, Frank Common, phoned. A most uncommon man is Frank Common. His vocation is law and his hobby is music, but his avocation is motivating and leading a group of thinkers dedicated to the concept that people the world over require information that will help them help themselves with problems and situations common to almost everyone.

Frank started our telephone conversation by saying that, no matter what he was about to relate, I should not suspect that he had become mentally unstuck. He was, he assured me, of sound mind and body, and if I would bear with him for a moment or two, I would comprehend the seemingly incomprehensible.

He said he was taking some holidays in order to make a study of electric organs, because he wanted to buy not one but two of a model which he would select for his particular needs. Frank, a talented pianist, explained that he already had in the music room of his home a Hammond organ, two Steinways, drums, and other musical instruments, but a whole new musical vista had recently opened to him. He was planning to move from his house into an apartment on the top floor of The Gleneagles, an old, castle-like structure on the slope of Westmount Mountain. Above the apartment, he had discovered a room that had never been used. Frank believed the room, with its vaulted ceiling twenty-seven feet high, would have ideal acoustic qualities. Therefore, he wanted to buy an organ with newly developed electronic devices that could be hooked up with his Hammond to produce unusual musical effects. In addition, he wanted a second organ to give to a friend on a special occasion.

Frank had visited most of Montreal's organ retailers including Simpsons, and had made a preliminary selection. Eaton's had on the floor of its Montreal store the model in which Frank was most interested, but the store did not seem as eager to sell as Frank was to buy. He therefore turned to Simpsons – and to me.

Eaton's was then, as now, Simpsons' principal rival, and for years I had been locked into a competitive war with the chain. Taking business, any business, from Eaton's, was one of my great delights. Later, I began to wonder if Eaton's lack of interest in the sale had been caused by a premonition of things to come, and if they were merely demonstrating their traditional business acumen by avoiding a distressing situation.

Frank's immediate request was that I obtain a manual for Lowrey organ model GAK, which Eaton's had declined to provide. I did. Overnight.

After Frank studied the manual, he became so interested in model GAK, that he decided it would be worth his while to go to Chicago and talk to the Lowrey people at their main office. Through a friend of his, Frank was introduced to Arnold M. Berlin, president of the Chicago Musical Instrument Company, of which Lowrey is a division.

Frank, his wife Katherine, and Lois Henderson, one of Montreal's best-known organists, journeyed to Chicago to tour the factory. Lowrey gave the group a royal reception and a short, but intensive week-end course in the designs and capabilities of Lowrey organs.

Frank phoned me on Monday to tell me that he had confirmed his choice and that he required at least the gift organ in Montreal by the following Saturday. Because time was so short he offered to pay air transportation charges.

I told Frank to leave the matter with me and that I would keep him advised on how things were proceeding. I phoned Chicago, briefed Lowrey's national sales manager, Donald Wennlund, on the details, and asked for his co-operation in expediting shipment. Experience had taught me to take nothing for granted, so I took care of all the ordering details personally.

I asked Mr. Wennlund to deliver the organs and necessary export papers to the Air Canada freight terminal in Chicago before eleven the following morning. I told him that our traffic department had made the necessary arrangements with Air Canada and that the carrier realized how urgent the shipment was.

On Tuesday, when my secretary told me that a telephone call from Air Canada in Chicago was being referred to me by our traffic department, I knew at once we were in trouble.

The Air Canada dispatcher told me that both organs were on the dock as scheduled, but that he could not load them because each carton bore a prominent label reading, "KEEP UPRIGHT. DO NOT LAY CARTON ON ITS SIDE." He went on to explain that the height of the freight compartment did not permit this method of shipping and that Air Canada could not accept responsibility for the shipment.

"Leave it to me," I told him. "I'll be back to you."

"Hurry," he replied. "We take off in less than an hour."

Don Wennlund was out to lunch; the Lowrey traffic manager referred my call to the engineering department; and while I was waiting to speak to engineering, Air Canada departed Chicago.

Back to Simpsons traffic department. There must be *some* way. Ah, yes! Air France had a 747 leaving Chicago for Montreal and

Paris every second day with plenty of height and room to position the organs any way the Lowrey people demanded.

The next flight was on Wednesday. The plane would arrive in Montreal Wednesday evening, leaving ample time for delivery.

On Wednesday, after being assured by Air France, Chicago, that the organs were indeed on the 747 bound for Montreal, I left for Toronto to attend a Simpsons board meeting on Thursday.

Shortly after the meeting began, it was interrupted to notify me that my secretary, Marie Rivet, was calling from Montreal with an urgent message.

"Mr. Bryant," she said, "I have done everything I can think of doing, but now I must tell you the bad news. The organs weren't unloaded in Montreal and are in Paris!"

What's more, Miss Rivet told me, French customs had impounded the organs because they had arrived, naturally, without proper documentation. She further explained that if they had not been impounded, the organs could have been shipped back to Montreal on the return flight which was about to depart Paris.

I directed Miss Rivet to telephone the chief executive officer of Air France and have him deal with French customs agents.

But that was a long shot, so about 11:00 a.m. I phoned Don Wennlund and explained the situation to him. (By this time, we were on a "Don" and "Jim" basis.) At least one organ had to be in Montreal the following day no matter what the cost.

With that, the Lowrey organization really went into high gear. Wesley Sharrat, one of their bright young senior engineers, owned a second-hand Ford Econoline truck. He arranged to take the gift organ to Montreal in it and, if he ran into trouble, to telephone directly to Frank Common. Wes called his wife, Joan, out of the school where she taught, hired a babysitter to take care of their children, and about nine o'clock on Thursday evening the two set out on the nine-hundred-mile trip to Montreal with the gift organ in the van. They arrived at the Windsor, Ontario border at about three o'clock Friday morning, where they explained to a startled Canadian customs officer that they must clear the organ through customs immediately.

At first it appeared that they would have to wait until 8:30 in the morning when a customs broker would be available, but the night man remembered that a woman broker, whom he identified only as

Marge, lived a short distance away and sometimes responded in emergencies. Marge agreed to come to the Sharrats' rescue. About 3:45 a.m., documentation completed, the couple resumed their trip.

Almost at once the van's motor began to act up but, as no garages were open, the Sharrats kept going at a painfully slow pace.

Finally, at four o'clock Friday afternoon, as they drove along Montreal's Côte de Liesse Boulevard toward the city's centre, the truck staggered to a halt. Sharrat called Frank and explained his plight. Frank jumped into his car and set off for Côte de Liesse.

As he drove frantically through the late afternoon traffic, Frank realized that he and Wes would need help to get the truck started, so he stopped at a Texaco station and picked up the owner, explaining the problem as they headed toward the broken-down van.

The service station owner thought that another truck might be required to transport the organ to its destination. Looking in the rear-view mirror he noticed that a supplier of his, Dick Finnerty of the Goodyear Tire and Rubber Company, was at the wheel of the panel truck immediately behind them.

Dick was minding his own business, driving home to dinner, when the Texaco dealer flagged him down and asked him to follow Frank's car.

When Finnerty, Frank, and the Texaco dealer reached the Sharrats' van, the four men decided to try to drive the Econoline to a large Ford truck service depot about a mile down the boulevard.

The centre's security setup included steel fence gates that closed at 5:00 p.m. on Fridays and could not be opened until 8:30 a.m. on Mondays. At about 4:55 p.m., the van, the truck, and Frank's car were wandering around the compound looking for someone with whom they could discuss servicing the Econoline. Suddenly, Dick Finnerty realized that the gates were about to close and impound the vehicles and the organ for the weekend. Hastily, they transferred the organ to the Goodyear truck, left the Econoline truck on the lot, and escaped from the compound seconds before the gates clamped shut.

When I was informed on Friday evening that the organ had arrived, my relief was boundless. Early Saturday morning I called Frank for a final check. At that moment, Wes Sharrat, the Lowrey engineer, Bill Parsons, Simpsons' organ expert, Lois Henderson, the organist, and the Simpsons delivery man were having coffee with him. All were waiting to transport the organ to the home of Philip Johnston. The furniture was to be rearranged and the installation made while Philip's wife had him out shopping on some pretext.

At ten o'clock, precisely as scheduled, a very surprised Johnston returned to a mighty musical greeting played by Lois Henderson on his new organ.

In the meantime, almost unnoticed, Air France had returned the two organs from Paris, and Frank's own instrument was delivered and installed that same morning.

Afterward, Frank invited my wife and me to a party he was hosting at Au Lutin Qui Bouffe, Montreal's famous "little pig" restaurant, in celebration of the happy ending. Before dinner, the Johnstons, the Sharrats, Lois Henderson, my wife, and I met at Frank's home and were escorted to the music room by Frank and Katherine. There, with Frank on the piano and Lois on the Lowrey, combining her playing with a tape she had made earlier and a device that simulated bagpipes, we enjoyed a jazzed-up version of "Loch Lomond," which would have tested the acoustics of Carnegie Hall.

Mission accomplished, Wes and Joan Sharrat were eager to return to Chicago. But the truck could not be repaired until Monday. To make the couple's enforced stay in Montreal more interesting, Frank gave them his tickets to the Stanley Cup playoff game the following day, between the Chicago Black Hawks and the Montreal Canadiens. Frank always selected seats behind the visiting players' bench because, from there, he could see the Canadiens attacking the enemy's net in two of the three periods. As a result, to the amazement of their Chicago friends, Wes and Joan Sharrat, sitting directly behind the Chicago bench, were on television much of the evening!

* * *

In the annals of accounting confusion, an error made by Simpsons in 1947 must surely be a classic.

At that time I was manager of a group of departments at Simpsons, Montreal; my brother-in-law, Sheldon Fraser of Edmonton, made frequent business visits to Montreal during this period. On one such trip, Sheldon purchased from Simpsons an Indian rug

45

priced at $495. I arranged to open a special charge account so that the store could bill him for this one purchase.

A month or two later, back in Montreal, Sheldon complained to me that our credit department was hounding him, despite the fact that he had paid the account and received from his bank his cancelled cheque endorsed and cashed by Simpsons. I called the credit department, listed the details, obtained assurance that everything was under control, and told Sheldon to ignore the dunning notices.

A month later, he remarked that perhaps our credit department could do with an efficiency expert. He was still being harassed. I registered another complaint and received another assurance that the error would be corrected.

On a later trip to Montreal, Sheldon came to my office in a state of downright anger. Now, he said, Simpsons was planning to turn over collection of his so-called account to its legal department.

At that point, I did what I should have done in the first place. Leaving Sheldon in my office, I stormed up to the credit manager's office and made it clear that the mistake must be rectified while I was there, and that I would not be subjected to further embarrassment.

Audit copies for special accounts like Sheldon's were filed alphabetically in small drawers, with a cardboard divider separating each account. In the Fraser section, however, there were, not one, but two audit slips. The first covered the purchase of a rug for $495 by my brother-in-law, who was listed as Mr. S. A. Fraser of Edmonton, Alberta. The second, a purchase in precisely the same amount, had been made by a member of the paper-making Fraser family of Edmundston, New Brunswick.

The credit manager solved the mystery by discovering that when my brother-in-law had mailed his cheque for $495 to Simpsons, he had neglected to include the fifteen-cent excise tax in force in Canada at that time. The fifteen-cent balance due had kept his account open. And, because his audit slip had been filed first, the billing clerk, who did not know Alberta from New Brunswick, let alone Edmonton from Edmundston, had assumed that the two audit slips constituted one account and persisted in sending bills and dunning notices to Sheldon Fraser of Edmonton.

* * *

During World War II, the Wartime Prices and Trade Board in Winnipeg was headed by a merchandiser named Young who had been lent to the government by the T. Eaton Company. Apparently Murphy's Law went with him. No one, ever, crossed Mr. Young willingly. In the summer of 1942, when the head office in Ottawa sent Young a man to administer consumer rationing which was soon to be introduced, Young sent him back to Ottawa on the next train and hired me, a fellow department store type, albeit from a rival company.

The new rationing organization's first task was to prepare coupon books to be issued to every man, woman, and child in Manitoba and north-western Ontario. The name of the holder had to be written on the face of each book, and the book's number recorded on a filing card. To inscribe names on the nearly one million books, two hundred school teachers on summer vacation were hired. They were put to work at the University of Manitoba, three blocks from the Wartime Prices and Trade Board offices in downtown Winnipeg.

I visited our university offices two or three times daily to check on the progress of the work and to make sure that all the books would be ready to mail before the date set to begin rationing sugar, tea, and coffee. On one of my visits, I discovered that the printer had delivered a large shipment of ration books containing extra sheets of green sugar coupons. When I informed Mr. Young, he was incensed, suggesting darkly that the additional coupons had been printed for black marketeers, but were accidentally bound into the ration books!

To prevent the extra coupons from being issued, more teachers were hired to inspect each book and extract the additional sheets. The offending coupons were then placed in large cartons, sealed, and burned once a day in the university's incinerator under the supervision of two ration administration employees.

One windy day shortly after the project began, I was walking across the university lawn on my way back to my office, when I came upon a sheet of sugar coupons lying on the grass. I picked it up in horror. Before I had time to wonder how it came there, I saw another. And another. And another. The lawn was green – with coupons!

The singed edges of some of the coupon sheets explained the mystery. High winds had caused a draught to rise through the incinerator chimney, propelling upward and outward thousands of sheets of sugar coupons.

I rushed back to the university office and, in minutes, three hundred teachers were scouring the university grounds, nearby parliament buildings, adjacent streets, lanes, backyards – every square inch of the area within two or three blocks of the incinerator. In all, we collected thousands of coupon sheets.

Satisfied at last that the best possible job had been done, I made my way apprehensively toward Mr. Young's office to explain to him what had happened. I had visions of reporters finding coupons and spreading the story all over the morning newspapers. I also believed that Mr. Young would fly into a rage. As I approached Mr. Young's door, the office manager, a fellow named McCowan, was just leaving.

"Is the old man in a good mood?" I asked.

"I would think not!" he exclaimed, causing my apprehension to increase markedly.

With some trepidation, I entered Young's office and described the events of the past hour. There was no outburst. Instead, Mr. Young quietly asked if I was sure that the teachers had done a good job of picking up the coupons.

"Yes, sir," I assured him, "I walked over the entire area myself. Not a coupon in sight."

With that, I was dismissed. As I exited, I bumped into McCowan. I told him how surprised I was at Mr. Young's reaction, or lack of reaction.

"It is possible," said McCowan, "that I softened him up before you got in to see him."

McCowan then explained that, on his way back from lunch a short time earlier, he had looked up to see a sheet of paper floating down toward the street from the general direction of our offices on the top floor of the Power Building. He had caught the paper before it touched the ground, read it, and discovered it to be a top-secret letter from Donald Gordon, chairman of the Wartime Prices and Trade Board, informing Young of the date on which tire rationing would be imposed.

Only minutes before McCowan had snatched the document out of the air, Mr. Young had received it, opened the envelope, read the letter, and placed it on his desk. He then walked into his private washroom. As he opened the office door, a strong breeze had whisked the letter off his desk, out the open window, and into the hands of McCowan on the street below. Until the office manager returned the letter, Young had not known that it had left his desk!

The Shoplifters

Like any other community, the department store has its share, perhaps more than its share, of dishonesty. Hold-up men, embezzlers, con artists, bribers, and common shoplifters attack from all sides. And like in a small town, it is usually well-known and often respected insiders who are responsible for the greatest financial losses.

Shoplifting is, for those outside department stores, the most interesting and the least understood of all goings-on in the business. It is also a fact that department store executives do not know that much about shoplifting either, no matter how knowing they claim to be.

For one thing, no one knows for sure the exact number of dollars shoplifters are responsible for in any given period of time, in any given store. Statistics are impressive. Newspapers quote astronomical figures – $250,000,000 in 1975 for Canada was a recent quotation for all retail stores, including supermarkets; more than ten times that for the US.

What they are talking about is inventory shrinkage, which may be vastly different from shoplifting. Inventory shrinkage can only be calculated by periodic stocktaking, that is, by physically counting every single item in a store on a day which ends a specific period (say six months), after the store has closed and sales have ceased to be made. (In practice, the stocktaking usually takes place over a number of days and various accounting devices are used to bring all the figures together as of the end of the final day's counting.)

Department stores use what is known as the retail method of inventory. The wholesale cost of a particular item ends up in the books as a percentage figure. The retail price alone is used for stock taking purposes. This system provides stores with a convenient and simple means of knowing what they should have in stock. If accurate records are kept of the stock on hand at, say, January 1, the additions made to this stock (known as purchases), the sales made to customers, and the markdowns taken on merchandise reduced because it did not sell at the original prices, the stock which should be on hand on, say, July 1, can be calculated.

Stock on hand in retail dollars on January 1, plus purchases, minus sales, minus markdowns (all made between January 1 and July 1), equal stock on hand at July 1 in retail dollars. The difference between this calculated figure and the amount of stock actually found in the store by the physical counting is the inventory shrinkage.*

It is obvious then, that more than shoplifting (defined as the stealing of merchandise from a store by an outsider posing as a customer) is responsible for the shrinkage. It is equally obvious that department store executives do not know for sure the precise amount of the total shrinkage to attribute to shoplifting, because dozens of other factors are involved in the discrepancy. One of these factors, a far greater problem in most department stores than shoplifting, is theft by employees of merchandise or money. One expert on prevention of crime by employees states that 70% of inventory shrinkage can be attributed to employees. He believes shoplifting accounts for only 15%, and bookkeeping errors are responsible for the remaining 15%.

Failure to accurately record markdowns also clouds the figures. If a store reduces 100 men's suits from $200 to $150 each, and does not enter this on its books, then $5000 would be missing from the inventory. Often, incorrect price tickets are placed on merchandise. If the wrong price ticket is too high, the merchandise rarely sells; if too low, it is swept off the counters by eager and knowing customers, and a stock shortage ensues.

Sometimes suppliers accidently ship smaller quantities of merchandise than are covered by the invoice. On rare occasions, the short shipment is deliberate. If this discrepancy is not caught by the store's receivers, the inventory shrinkage is again increased.

Shipping errors help bring on inventory shortages (and attacks of

---

* Some stores, mostly food stores, use the cost method of inventory. Stocktaking is made, using the actual cost of the merchandise. Shrinkage then shows up as a lower than expected percentage of gross profit.

department store disease). If the store's customer does not receive all the merchandise he is being charged for, a complaint is certain to result; but this is not always the case when something is received that has not been paid for, since stores only know of overshipments reported by honest customers, fortunately the vast majority.

The potential magnitude of the problem was illustrated to me when I was general manager of Simpsons' Halifax store. One Saturday morning a telephone call from a frantic woman was relayed to me. She was almost hysterical when I came on the phone. "Mr. Bryant, please don't tell me that I am in the right church but the wrong pew. I know I should be talking to Simpsons-Sears," she began. "But there is no one at Simpsons-Sears today (mail-order people never worked Saturdays), and I need help."

Some weeks earlier, she told me, she had ordered from Simpsons-Sears' catalogue a doll carriage for her small daughter's birthday. To avoid disappointment, she had ordered well ahead of the date. The carriage arrived in what seemed to be an overly large carton. Her apartment, on the upper floor of a house, was approached by a small landing with a low, sloping ceiling. The carton took up most of the floor area and pushed against the ceiling. For a week or so, while awaiting the birthday festivities, she, her husband, and two small children had to squeeze by the carton (which was left unopened to conceal its contents) in order to enter or leave the apartment. When the carton was eventually opened, it was found to contain not one, but six doll carriages. Simpsons-Sears was informed of the error and requested to pick up the surplus. Thinking that, like most complaints, the call was to inform them of non-receipt of merchandise ordered, Simpsons-Sears promptly sent out another carton of six doll carriages. The woman was out when it arrived, so the driver left it in the downstairs hall, where it interfered with opening the door and annoyed the downstairs tenants.

The second time the woman explained her problem more carefully to the complaint department, so carefully, in fact, that it took about a week to get through the routine, while tempers were rising upstairs and down. Finally, about an hour before she got me on the phone, a Simpsons driver (Simpsons and Simpsons-Sears used the same delivery system) arrived at her door. Was he there to pick up the two unwanted cartons? Not at all. He was there with another carton of six. What's more, he knew the rules. He would deliver parcels on his truck, but he would not pick up items unless he had a call card – the voucher used to document returns made by customers through the delivery system. The third carton was left on the stairs, but soon slipped down and blocked the entrance door completely.

"I cannot put up with this any longer," she cried, "and if you can't help me, the latest carton is going on the front lawn. In fact, all three cartons will end up on the front lawn." I thanked her on behalf of Simpsons-Sears, and sent a truck to pick up the cartons within the hour. On Monday, I asked the Simpsons-Sears people how the stock shortages were going in the toy department.

With such antics creating stock shortages, it is not surprising that department stores can only guess at the proportion of the shrinkage attributable to shoplifting. One thing they do know, however, is that it is more of a problem in 1976 than it was in 1946. They know also that thefts by shoplifters and store employees are increasing at an alarming rate, because total inventory shrinkage* grows with each passing year, while the non-criminal sources of losses are fairly steady.

Increased shoplifting is caused in part by stores themselves and in part by changing life styles. Stores aid and abet shoplifters by using self-selection or self-service operating methods. And department store executives who allow themselves to be misled by store planners and designers are almost guaranteeing that shoplifting losses will be high. In their efforts to emulate Neiman-Marcus and Bonwit Teller by creating beautiful shops, many designers so compartmentalize new stores that they are constructed as series of ridiculously small areas, blocked off from and so unrelated to each other that the poor customer has no way of knowing whether he is in Bloomingdale's or Saks, Simpsons or Eaton's – or Korvettes.

The Hudson's Bay Company created a shoplifters' paradise in a new store in the Montreal suburb of Dorval. The men's furnishings department, with barely enough space in the shop for clerks and cus-

---

* The rate of increase is dramatized by these statistics. Inventory shrinkage for Canadian department stores expressed as a percentage of sales, increased from 1.1% in 1965 to 1.7% in 1970. Sales in 1965 were $1,910,836,000. In 1970 these had increased to $2,852,320,000. This means that in just five years dollar losses more than doubled from $21,019,196 to $48,489,440. (Figures supplied by the Retail Council of Canada.)

tomers at the same time, resembled a cage in a zoo – a high-class zoo to be sure, but a zoo nevertheless. This problem was compounded by a lack of salespeople, as scarce in some stores as colours and sizes.

Shortly after the store was opened, I watched a customer with a belt in his hand walking around the men's shop like a monkey waiting for his keeper to relieve him of a banana peel. Then I toured the building. About half an hour later, I returned to the men's department. The customer with the belt was still there. Perhaps he gave up eventually and walked out, belt in hand. I was not surprised to learn a short time later that the store had installed a closed-circuit TV system to control the activities of customers whose presence could not be detected by other means.

While stores have been making it easier to steal, the public's attitude has changed, too. Shoplifting is no longer considered to be a serious crime by many who believe themselves to be honest citizens. Many young people think of it as some kind of game in which the most successful is classed with the local football hero. Stealing school rings from a downtown department store became quite as important to some girl students of a posh Toronto private school as passing exams. The most dangerous offender, however, is the drug user. Selling stolen merchandise is the most common, often the only, way that addicts are able to support their habit.

But, things are getting tougher for those who steal from stores. Many will learn what they should have known all along – that shoplifting is just as much a crime as holding up a bank. Stores are taking a much harder line than they did a few years ago.

At one time there was an amazing reluctance to prosecute shoplifters. Some even thought the publicity would hurt the store. The newspapers obligingly referred to thefts as having taken place in a "downtown department store." It never seemed to occur to management that the publicity might have some benefit, for if thieves found better assortments in their store than in a competitor's establishment, customers might do likewise. (In fact, police records tend to show that thieves' preferences for stores are about the same as that of legitimate customers'.) While shoplifters were rarely prosecuted, employees, for practical purposes, never were. Although store managements are more outraged by employees stealing than by customers stealing, they usually knew the employee personally and for that reason refrained from prosecuting.

55

During the period when shoplifters were being handled with kid gloves, kleptomania was very much in fashion. Many a confirmed thief was able to hide behind this so-called disease. Often stores were ready, if not eager, to accept the defence, for the confession was always accompanied by full and prompt restitution.

True kleptomania must be extremely rare. Moreover, it is an ailment that never seems to afflict the poor. Personally, I have known only two cases that could be substantiated: a prominent doctor's wife, and a minister's wife. In the first case a member of the investigation staff would begin following the woman as soon as she entered the store. He would make a list of pilfered merchandise, which would range from cheap souvenirs, ridiculous in her social situation, to useful, valuable items such as leather handbags. A statement, sent to the woman's husband, was always promptly paid. In the second case, the minister himself followed his wife and made up his own list. He either paid for or returned the purloined goods.

With inventory losses skyrocketing because of thefts by shoplifters and employees, prosecution by stores has now become the rule rather than the exception.

Although prosecution is felt to be the only way to reduce theft from stores, many offenders are still not brought before the courts. Today, however, the reasons for not prosecuting make some sense.

It seemed unwise, for example, to prosecute the fellow who was picked up in a Simpsons Montreal store with a number of bottles of perfume, figurines, and other loot – he turned out to be the bishop of a suburban diocese. Occasionally a woman is picked up who turns out to be a nun not in her usual garb. A Montreal police captain's wife was released because the theft was small and would not justify the embarrassment to her husband. The decision turned out to be both wise and fortuitous. Simpsons now has a friend at police headquarters who has been most helpful in expediting the work of store investigators.

Well-run department stores invariably send home youngsters apprehended for the first time, in the custody of their parents. Often both parent and child end up with a lasting benefit – the child with an unforgettable lesson, and the parent with the knowledge that his indifference may have contributed to the youngster's unfortunate behaviour.

Such was the case when the fourteen-year-old son of a highly respected judge was picked up in Simpsons after he had outfitted himself with a complete wardrobe. His father was persuaded to recess his court in order to take a telephone call relating to an important family matter. The recess was continued while the judge rushed to his son's side. The boy cried; the father cried. But the father realized that his devotion to his responsibilities in administering justice had interfered with his relationship with his son. The two left the store's investigation office with an entirely new friendship.

Occasionally department store security people bring to justice persons responsible for crimes committed elsewhere. A Simpsons' executive in Toronto was robbed of a valuable stamp collection when his home was broken into. The executive often browsed through stamp stores during lunch hours. Shortly after the break-in he caught a glimpse of a familiar book which was being shown to the owner of one of these stores. As he approached the counter, the man with the book of stamps left and mingled with the crowd on the street. A few words with the owner established that they were indeed the executive's stamps being offered for sale. Annoyed that the thief had escaped, he made his way to his office in Simpsons. As he was passing the stamp counter he noticed the same man offering the stamps to Simpsons' stamp buyer. After calling the security people to notify the police, he sidled up to the man at the counter about the time the buyer was rejecting the offer. The executive said that since Simpsons was not interested he might consider a direct purchase. His inspection of the stamps was prolonged until he was certain Simpsons' investigators and the city police were present. The would-be stamp vendor turned out to be a city fireman who had an avocation as a housebreaker on his days off.

In London, Ontario, the credit manager became suspicious of a private nurse who had been authorized by her patient to make personal purchases for him on his Simpsons account. The patient was ill and elderly. It was interesting therefore that the nurse was buying a wide range of merchandise that he was unlikely to use. A security check revealed that the woman had worked in London, England as a nurse and she was wanted in that city for making fraudulent purchases on an elderly patient's charge account. Some habits are hard to break.

In Halifax, a shoplifter walked off with a portable TV. Made by Philips, it was operated by batteries and housed in a handsome leather case, as portable for shoplifters as customers. It was also very expensive – four hundred dollars in the 1950s. The department manager told the police that the distinctive battery required to operate the set had been removed. He suggested that someone would soon order such a battery from Philips. That someone would, of course, be the thief or a fence to whom the thief had sold the set. His prediction turned out to be correct. Within a few days the fence who ordered the battery was surprised to have it delivered by a detective. The fence was convicted along with the thief.

Some thieves disappear completely and cannot be prosecuted. Four days before Simpsons began attaching a photograph of each new employee to their application form, a young woman walked into the employment office of Simpsons' Montreal store. It was a Friday at the height of the Christmas season. She was, she said, an experienced cashier and had worked for Simpsons in Toronto. She explained that she had recently married a Montreal university student and was available for work during the Christmas rush. A brief test confirmed that she was indeed an experienced cashier. Saturday morning at 9 a.m., she was assigned to the men's furnishings department, the busiest section in the store. She worked there until 5:30 p.m., when the store closed. She was to report for work again on Monday morning at 9 a.m., but did not. About that time, the head cashier was informed that the cash bags for her register, containing some $5,000, could not be found. They were never again seen – nor was the cashier. She may have been seen but not recognized, for no one could remember a thing about her. She might have been tall or short, blonde or brunette. That afternoon Simpsons began taking pictures.

That was not one of Simpsons' better Christmas seasons for theft control. A week or two earlier, two fellows who claimed to be on Christmas vacation from a Kingston, Ontario college, were hired to drive delivery trucks. They took their trucks, fully loaded with Christmas parcels, onto the streets of Montreal on a snowy December day – and disappeared. A day later, the trucks, minus their contents, were found parked on isolated side streets. No one could remember much about the men. Through their employment application cards it was established that they were indeed from Kingston; however they had not been attending the "college of their choice" but were recently released from the penitentiary. Some months later, another caper in Vancouver ended in their return to Kingston for another semester.

Once in a while store security people have little desire to apprehend a thief, and no stomach whatsoever to recover the stolen goods. A lucrative shoplifter's ploy is stealing parcels, which customers inadvertently leave on counters while contemplating further purchases. The filcher operates in relative safety, because the stolen merchandise is concealed in the store's box or bag, and some time usually passes before the loss is discovered. Women's washrooms in stores are also regular targets of these operators.

In Simpsons' Montreal store a few years ago, a rash of such thefts occurred. At first, full shopping bags were frequently stolen, although these soon became less popular than other parcels because, before the advent of the plastic garbage bag, a sensitive Simpsons executive decided that, for reasons of delicacy, women porters should use Simpsons shopping bags rather than brown paper bags to remove the unflushables from the women's washrooms.

On occasion, a customer may walk away with merchandise without realizing what is happening. One rainy day in The Bay in Winnipeg, when I worked in the linen department, I rushed to a nearby escalator landing, where a woman was screaming hysterically. I naturally assumed that there had been an accident on the escalator, but the shopper was agitated for other reasons. She had been one of a horde of shoppers attacking a sale of knitting yarns heaped on tables in the art needlework department. She found nothing in the sale she wished to buy, but she was certain she would be accused of shoplifting because as she was about to board the escalator she noticed, to her horror, one ball of yarn impaled on almost every spoke of her umbrella.

Now and then overzealous security staff catch someone they never should have caught. When persons taken into custody because a security investigator observed (or thought he observed) a theft, do not have the suspect item on their person, the store is immediately threatened with a suit for false arrest. All department stores carry insurance against this eventuality, and the matter is immediately turned over to an adjuster. Suits are more often threatened than carried out, and few reach the courts. Usually the case is resolved by a small cash settlement, or, occasionally, by a letter (which does not admit liability) expressing the store's regret that the incident occurred.

The most frequent reason for quick, painless settlements is that the presumed theft was made by a person who *does* have a police record as a shoplifter, realizes he is under observation and manages to dispose of the pilfered item before being taken into custody. Sometimes, while negotiations regarding the false arrest charge are taking place, these people "blow their case" by being caught red-handed shoplifting in the same store.

While stores accused of false arrest usually get off the hook when a shoplifter with a record is involved, it is not as difficult as may be supposed to deal with those who do not have a record. This is because the suspected person usually *has* made a theft, although the merchandise has somehow or other been disposed of before the apprehension takes place. And occasionally, the potential thief has a change of heart. In such cases, a lawsuit is frequently avoided by suggesting to the claimant that some unfortunate revelations may take place in court. A settlement representing a mere fraction of the original claim is the likely result, or the suit is dropped completely.

Such was the case when a Halifax policeman's son of thirteen was picked up in Simpsons. He had been observed pocketing a piece of jewelry, but had disposed of it when an investigator momentarily lost sight of him as they moved through the crowded store. The embarrassed security man released the boy, and advised me that I could expect a visit from his father. He was right. The following morning an irate policeman was in my office, loudly threatening to take Simpsons through every court in the land. Trying not to show my nervousness, I suggested that he either calm down and talk to me, or use his prerogative and talk to his lawyer. When quiet prevailed, I said: "Look, as a policeman, you surely appreciate that we do not apprehend suspects without just cause. I have a full report from our investigator, and I am satisfied that he had ample reason to be suspicious. If you sue, your son will be called on to give testimony and he will be questioned by a most inquiring and experienced trial lawyer. Would you like to expose him to that? Might not some embarrassing details be revealed?" The policeman became thoughtful. "Why don't you have another chat with your son?" I suggested. "He may not have told you the full story. I, too, am a father, and believe me, I am sympathetic."

That afternoon he called and told me that I was right. The boy had picked up the piece of jewelry as a prank, but had disposed of it when he realized he was being watched. He sincerely appreciated that he had been able to provide his son with a relatively painless, hopefully permanent, lesson.

What I did not tell the policeman was that I, too, had learned a lesson that helped me resolve similar situations in the future; when he entered my office I was as upset as he was, and had no idea whatsoever of what I would say or do.

But the headlong rush by stores, especially limited service or discount stores, to prosecute anybody and everybody suspected of shoplifting has been slowed perceptibly by two recent court awards for false arrest. One was made in Canada, the other in the US, and in keeping with the size of the two countries the US judgement was over ten times that brought down in Canada.

The Canadian case resulted in the largest false arrest award ever made by a Canadian court, as far as insurance executives who handle such cases, can remember.

On April 26, 1974, the Supreme Court of Ontario awarded Annie Yarek, $82,601 for false arrest and defamation of character. She was apprehended in the Allied Towers discount store in Brantford and accused of theft in the presence of other shoppers. It turned out to be a costly case of mistaken identity.

In the United States, at about the same time, it cost the Korvette department store's Brooklyn branch an astronomical $1,100,000 for persisting in the prosecution of a young woman for shoplifting, without witnesses or evidence to support the charge. Laureen Bernstein was a twenty-year-old bank teller when she was apprehended by store security officers and accused of helping Puerto Rican girls steal merchandise from the store. The girls, who were being held in the store's security office, denied knowing her and, although no stolen items were found on her person, and the police sergeant who booked her at the store's insistence warned of a possible false arrest charge, Korvettes persisted in prosecuting. She was acquitted and promptly sued Korvettes. Her attorney was able to establish that the physical apprehension in the store, the removal to the police station, and the insistence on the part of the store to prosecute had caused Miss Bernstein severe psychological trauma which would require continued treatment. She was awarded $500,000 in compensatory damages and $600,000 in punitive damages, presumably because of the store's vindictiveness.

While Towers and Korvettes were learning painful lessons, bound to result in modifying their security tactics, it remained for Simpsons in Montreal to come up with what must be the most absurd case of false arrest. Simpsons "Dunhill Humidor" keeps on hand expensive Cuban cigars, which have been specially ordered in large quantities for a select clientele. These are paid for on arrival and then stored in a room with precisely controlled temperature and humidity to keep the cigars fresh and moist until required. Each customer has his own locked compartment, rather like a bank safety deposit box, in which he keeps his private stock of personally selected cigars.

A few years ago, a well-to-do, highly respected Montreal businessman and philanthropist walked out of the Dunhill Shop onto St. Catherine Street. He was followed by an experienced staff investigator. On the street, the investigator hailed a Montreal police car. She identified herself and requested assistance in making an arrest. The police car proceeded slowly up the street, keeping pace with the investigator who, in turn, was a few steps behind the suspect. Eventually, the man was taken into custody. Outraged, he was taken back to the store, where he not only established his identity, but at once proved to the two policemen and a thoroughly embarrassed investigator that he had not been stealing. What he had done was to take some of his own cigars from his own compartment in the Dunhill Humidor. When the investigator saw him thrust a handful of cigars into the inside pocket of his suit coat, he was caught "stealing" his own property. Threat of a horrendous lawsuit was the inevitable consequence. But the man turned out to be both businesslike and reasonable. He realized that Simpsons' mistake resulted from unusual circumstances, and a reasonable settlement was agreed upon.

Despite an occasional setback through false arrest, confirmation of stores' determination to make life tougher for shoplifters is provided by a Toronto judge. He points out that on an average day in 1976 close to half the cases in the women's courts involve shoplifting, many times the proportion of a few years ago. He also confirms that shoplifting is primarily a woman's game, and relatively few men are accused of this offence.

While stores are bringing more shoplifters (as well as thieving employees) before the courts than in past years, department store executives and a Toronto judge who handles many shoplifting cases, believe that, on the whole, the courts are less severe than they were, say, twenty years ago and that indifference to shoplifting on the part of stores has been replaced, to some extent, by leniency by the courts. It would seem that the courts have, to a degree, gone along with our changing life style by showing leniency, especially to first offenders, which frequently arouses the ire of store security people. But judges are faced with much more difficult situations today than in past years. Youngsters from broken homes, or homes which lack parental supervision because both parents are working, require the sympathy of a judge with a social conscience. Immigrants who, for the first time in their lives, are exposed to vast displays of merchandise on self-selection fixtures, may well be given sympathetic hearings on a first offence. And even the most hardened of department store security men generally agree that it serves no useful purpose to be tough on the drunk who steals a pair of socks to trade for a bottle of cheap wine.

One problem for the courts is that offenders and their defence lawyers have developed a long list of more sophisticated excuses than those used in the past. While a few still claim to be compulsive thieves, or kleptomaniacs, today's excuse is more likely to be a depressed state of mind brought on by menopause, the menstrual cycle, post-natal worries, loss of memory, and countless other states of mind. These reasons, along with the time-worn ones of hardship and falling in with bad companions, make judging today's cases increasingly complex. And, of course, there are often character witnesses.

The parade of such witnesses is often long, and usually boring. But Judge Joseph Addison of the Ontario Provincial Court remembers at least one case that ended in a bit of levity. A boy's mother was the last of a long list of character witnesses supporting her son's honesty and integrity. She brought the case to a close with this remarkable statement: "Why, judge, this boy is so honest he brings home everything he steals."

Regardless of what happens in the courts, the retailer's objective is to reduce theft by shoplifters and by employees. Most shoplifting can be controlled by store management, because this type of larcency has physical limitations. Unless a store is almost completely lacking in supervision, shoplifters, except in collusion with store employees, can remove from a store only limited amounts of mer-

63

chandise. Of course, when items of high value and small size, cameras and real jewelry, for example, are displayed at exposed locations such as mall entrances, higher than normal losses can be expected.

In my experience, Simpsons in Halifax was the only store in which shoplifters were almost as successful as dishonest employees. The building had been designed originally as a mail-order distribution centre. The second floor, because of the slope of the land, was used to receive merchandise from manufacturers and to ship parcelled items to customers. Then, as customers started coming to the building for mail-order clearances, a retail business developed. Eventually, it was necessary to assign the main and third floors to retail activities, leaving the floor in between for mail-order functions. There were no escalators, and elevators were the only practicable means by which customers and employees could move from one level to another. Shoplifters found this layout most convenient and exploited it to the fullest.

The thieves were incredibly bold, and often worked in groups. One segment of a gang created a disturbance on the third floor to distract the security force, while other members, working on the main floor, reached into showcases and made off with cameras and binoculars. Occasionally, a security man would reach the theft scene in time. One shoplifter was chased out of the store and ended up waist-deep in the Atlantic Ocean's nearby North-West Arm. The investigator sat on shore smoking while the cold Atlantic waters assisted the capture. But most raids were so well planned that nearby salespeople could only watch in helpless amazement.

Probably the most frustrating aspect of these activities was that the participants who created diverting commotions were not intimidated by our efforts to force them to leave the premises, perhaps because Halifax courts were lenient, and it was often difficult to obtain convictions against shoplifters with what we felt was most compelling evidence.

Eventually these escapades were stopped by a simple tactic. One day, when I was particularly angered by one of the shoplifting gangs, it occurred to me that if we took photographs of the culprits we could at least show the pictures to the courts in cases of future apprehensions, since the offenders were indeed the same people who had harassed us on previous occasions. On the pretense of taking photographs of displays, we "shot" our molesters at point-blank range. It worked like magic. We were seldom bothered again by the persons who had been photographed.

The photography device had its limitations, however, for it was only useful on people whose activities were obviously suspicious, and the most common shoplifter – the one who casually picks up an item, puts it into a shopping bag or handbag, or thrusts it inside clothing – found Simpsons' Halifax store, the largest in the city, with huge columns and odd passageways (resulting from additions to the mail-order building) to hide behind or duck into, a particularly rewarding place to ply his trade. As a result, Simpsons' Halifax stock shortage was so much greater than at any other store in our company that my incipient stomach ulcers threatened to develop into the real thing. Our next-door neighbour in those days was Dr. Clarence Gosse, then one of Canada's foremost surgeons, now Lieutenant Governor of Nova Scotia. Clary knew what kind of a day I had had by the way I slammed the garage door. When the slamming was particularly emphatic, he would appear at his back door, glasses in hand, and announce that as a medical man he would recommend something to settle my nerves.

Later at dinner, I would entertain my family by relating a new story about a shoplifter or an employee who had been caught with his hand in the till. So it is not surprising that my wife subsequently got into the act by becoming, involuntarily, a store detective.

In Halifax, a port city, an efficient system for the distribution of stolen goods had developed. When television came to town, thieves found a ready market for sets which had been stolen from homes and stores.

One evening, with some anguish, I reported to my family that two portable television sets had been stolen that day from the selling floor. No one knew when or how the theft had been accomplished.

A few days later, my wife was about to board an elevator to shop on the third floor of our store. She noticed a woman, accompanied by a small child, struggling off the elevator with a not-too-portable, portable television. My wife's first thought was that someone working in the TV department should have carried the poor soul's purchase to her car. A few minutes later, however, as she stood on the upward-bound elevator, a question suddenly flashed across her mind: Was the set being stolen? She rushed from the elevator to my office and, as I was not there, told her story to Dave Campbell, the merchandise manager. Together they hurried to the TV department. The set had been stolen but, until then, had not been missed.

By that time, of course, the thief was well away from the store, but my wife was able to furnish a fairly accurate description of her. Later the same day, the suspect was spotted on the main floor. By the time the security man reached the scene, however, she had picked up a fur coat and headed for the parking lot. She was seen boarding a pick-up truck which drove off before she could be accosted, but not before the licence number had been noted by the security officer.

That evening, when the truck returned to its registered address, the woman and her male companion were taken into custody by waiting police. The television and the coat had been sold to a fence. Both fence and thief were tried and convicted, and the stolen articles found their way back to the store.

*   *   *

One of the most fascinating thieves in my experience was a fairly ordinary housewife.

When I became general manager of Simpsons' Halifax store in 1954, a most unusual situation existed in the credit department. For a year or so, fraudulent purchases were being made on two charge accounts. These first came to light when the legitimate account-holders complained they were being charged for purchases that they had not, in fact, made. Both were able to establish that the signatures on the sales slips which were sent with their monthly statements were forgeries. Neither had any idea how his credit card had come into the hands of a thief.

All the machinery normally used to apprehend this particular brand of crook was put into motion. Notices showing exact reproductions of the credit cards involved and the signatures which were being fraudulently used were sent to all salespeople and posted at cash stations.

Yet purchases continued. The credit department began to examine the accounts each month, the phoney sales slips were removed, and the amounts owing adjusted before the statements were mailed. Eventually, new account numbers were assigned to the customers, who then had no idea that forged purchases were continuing.

Early in the investigation, it had been established that the same elusive person was using both plates. She made purchases with great care, using first one account, then the other, buying at busy times from obviously inexperienced salespeople, in amounts low enough that the purchase would not be referred to the credit department for approval.

Nevertheless, as month followed month and year followed year and the stack of sales slips in this special account grew and grew, the dollar amount became substantial. Failure to catch this thief was a source of constant embarrassment to Don Whiting, head of security. At quiet times, he sometimes thumbed through the stack of bills and then threw them down in utter frustration. One day he noted that the thief had taken to buying two cartons of cigarettes regularly, at about three-week intervals. The personnel of the tobacco department were alerted and a signalling system worked out so that security people could be notified within a matter of seconds after either of the credit cards was presented for the purchase of cigarettes.

The first attempt to apprehend the crook failed because the security department did not respond quickly enough. But the sales clerk, a sixteen-year-old girl who had been assigned to relief work in the department a short time before, was composed enough to handle the situation without arousing the suspicions of the forger. At the same time, she got an excellent description of the wanted person.

The next time around, the woman was picked up. She was the wife of a man who held a responsible position with one of the Halifax utility companies. It was never determined whether or not he knew of his wife's activities but, in order to pay off the "special account" which by now amounted to some seven thousand dollars, the couple sold their home and dipped into their savings.

In this case, I was persuaded to forego prosecution, perhaps because it was such a relief to have the "special" charge account case behind us!

*   *   *

Every once in a while a superstar of the shoplifting world is nabbed. Often the apprehension is brought about not so much by design on the part of store security people as by accident and with

67

some help from a young salesperson, new on the job, enthusiastic and observant, who has not yet developed those set ways that professional shoplifters find so easy to take advantage of. My first experience with a truly big-time shoplifter was brought about by such circumstances.

Early in 1938, when I was assistant manager of the dress fabrics department of the Hudson's Bay Company's Winnipeg store, the store detective was a fellow named Dargie. He was the prototype of the department store dick that in a later era would regale television audiences. A typical flatfoot, he would hide behind the store's huge columns, dashing from one to the next in pursuit of his quarry. Watching Dargie was a favourite pastime of salespeople in those depression days – after all, there were not many customers to distract them. Sometimes the only person to be seen in a particular department, other than store employees, was Dargie's suspect. One day I was walking through the store with a fellow trainee, Wally Landreth, now vice-chairman of Canada's tariff board. We laughed quietly at Dargie, until we realized that the object of his attention was Wally's brother, Cam. It was with some relief that we realized that Cam was merely inspecting in great detail the features and figure of a comely young lady demonstrating cosmetics.

But Dargie did end up by recovering if not the largest, perhaps the most unusual, collection of stolen merchandise in department store history. One day I received a message that Mr. Dargie would like to see me in his office. His office was at the end of a long, narrow mezzanine floor stretching about one hundred feet along one side of the store. Dozens of tables, usually required for merchandise samples, were spread out along the outer wall of the store, leaving only a narrow aisle to Dargie's office. Every square foot of table was used to show an array of merchandise sufficient to stock two or three general stores. Items from almost every department were included: cups and saucers, large platters, silver flatware and hollow-ware, cutwork tablecloths, linens, all manner of clothing, clocks and watches, leaned against each other haphazardly.

As I made my way down the aisle I noted with some consternation two bolts of printed silk, recently arrived from New York, that were desperately needed back on the selling floor. Mr. Dargie was about to get a piece of my mind. I assumed he had removed the fabrics from the department for some purpose which, whatever it was, would not be sufficiently important to justify the loss of sales which would ensue. But Dargie did not give me an opportunity to chastise him. Instead, he led me back to the bolts of fabric and asked me to identify them as belonging to my department.

He then waved at the display down the aisle and, as I looked on in utter amazement at the hundreds of items on the tables, unfolded the story. Yes, they had all been stolen, even the bolts of fabric. What is more, they had all been stolen by one rather small, nondescript woman. They had been stolen over a period of at least twelve years. Some china items had the original price stickers placed on them by Robinsons, a Winnipeg department store which had closed in 1926; the fabrics had been stolen a few days earlier from The Bay. In between, every store of any importance in Winnipeg was represented. As usual, Eaton's was the favourite. Was this then the classic case of the kleptomaniac – the compulsive thief who steals for the sake of stealing? Not at all. This commonplace woman was a dope addict! For twelve years or more, her shoplifting had supported her habit. She simply returned to the stores enough merchandise to provide needed cash. She squirreled away the surplus around her home.

The detective showed me the drug paraphernalia she had used – a teaspoon, a small burner with a wick, a hypodermic syringe – which had been recovered from her house along with the merchandise. (Why everything ended up at The Bay, rather than in a police station, is somewhat difficult to comprehend.) The merchandise had been concealed all over the house – in cupboards, drawers, the attic, the basement, the garage. It took hours to assemble the loot. Yet the woman's husband, who had a good position with a large Winnipeg company, maintained that he knew absolutely nothing of his wife's activities. Given the magnitude of the operation, it was a most unlikely story.

But how could she elude store detectives for years and years? How could she physically move out of store premises thousands of items, weighing in total several tons, without being noticed by a single store employee? And why would the now embarrassed refund officials and auditors not notice that the same person was applying for cash refunds without benefit of sales slips every other day or so? For it is obvious that she would have to return about as many items as she had kept.

Time has blurred memories of the total amount of the defalcation;

a total of $36,000 over the twelve years seems possible. I leave the reader to translate 1938 dollars into today's values. How then could an operation of this magnitude go unnoticed? The answer is that she had no special methods, no unique techniques, no sophisticated equipment. She did not plan her thefts, and did not care whether anyone was watching. She simply went to a counter or a display, picked up an item, large or small, walked out of the store with it, placed in in her car, and drove home.

On the day of her last caper she chose a display of silver flatware. A young salesperson, her very first day on the job, saw the woman pick up a full chest and walk toward a Portage Avenue door. The youngster followed the customer, screaming at the top of her voice. Dargie, lurking for an entirely different purpose behind a pillar between the thief and the doorway, jumped out to ascertain what the commotion was all about. The woman with the chest of silver stumbled into his arms, her long career ended by sheer accident.

In the average department store, significant reductions in losses are not being achieved because security personnel are concentrating on the wrong people. Merchandise concealed in shopping bags, oversize bloomers, maternity clothes, double girdles with kangaroo-style pouches, and cleverly designed packages with false bottoms or sides which spring closed after the pilfered item is pushed inside, may make intriguing reading or television material, but when significant shrinkages occur, insiders, often in responsible management positions, are more likely to be the culprits.

What kinds of employees are likely to be or become thieves? There is, of course, no pattern. They may be young or old. They may begin stealing on their first day at work or shortly before retirement. There are, however, some signals that should arouse the suspicions of security personnel; an employee who is overly solicitous with a senior executive; one who comes in early and stays late, especially when carrying a large tote bag; a salesperson who serves the same customer almost daily (noon hour is the best time to watch); one who rarely takes vacations; the female who is picked up after work by a flashy-looking boy friend; one who appears to live beyond the income provided by the store. Charles Stewart, deputy chairman of Simpsons, tells of fingering a night watchman who mentioned trading in his car every year. A well-proportioned salesgirl in Simpsons downtown Montreal store explained her apparent affluence by claiming to double as a call girl in the evenings – a claim that may well have been true, but she also turned out to be a thief.

Ultimately, however, there is only one sure way to control stealing from a store: wage all-out war. And, make certain that customers with larceny in mind, as well as every employee – full-time, part-time, male, female, salesperson, driver, stockman, office worker, porter, every last one – knows that a war is on. Moreover, penalties imposed on enemies, whether employees or outsiders, must be as severe as the law permits. As I learned in Halifax, everyone connected with the store must be in battle dress, including the manager's wife!

But even the most sophisticated store executives are frequently surprised at the imagination and ingenuity displayed by dishonest employees, and grudgingly admire the new and unique methods these insiders devise to take money and merchandise, use customers' charge accounts, arrange kickbacks from suppliers, and steal through any system, no matter how foolproof it is supposed to be. Today, with electronics to do the dirty work, I fully expect to learn one day soon that a store has been bilked of many thousands of dollars by a cunning nocturnal computer expert.

Some of the most interesting inside thieves Simpsons had to deal with worked in the Montreal store in the forties and fifties.

Inventory losses of considerable amounts were cropping up all over the store but mostly in the big-ticket departments: men's suits, radios, floor coverings, and the like. Usually, significant shortages are confined to a few departments, and it is relatively simple to narrow down the suspects, but this was different, as many departments were being hit. It seemed that our thief had access to all departments – a cashier, a porter, or an exchange person. Even a nightwatchman. After all, nightmares of department store executives are frequently based on a single theme: "Who is watching the watchers?" (The nightmare became a reality at Eaton's Don Mills store in 1970 when the head of security was accused of heading up a ring which embezzled an estimated $100,000.)

At the time, the Montreal store was still using a pneumatic-tube system for processing most cash transactions. The money taken from the customer was placed in a tube, together with the sales slip and then carried through a conduit system to a cash room located in the sub-basement. The location of the thefts narrowed to this cash room.

Somehow, one of the cashiers, or perhaps a group of them, had found a way to steal cash sent through the system and to conceal these activities from the accountants and auditors. The personal lives of all the cashiers were quietly investigated, and a prime suspect turned up immediately. She was a statuesque blonde who, for some unfathomable reason, had been placed by the personnel people in the darkest dungeon in the building.

Perhaps this should not be surprising. Over the years, in various management responsibilities, I had a running battle with personnel departments because so little imagination was used in the placing of new employees. I felt sure our customers often wonder why doddering old dears who were skiing about the time the first ski tow went into operation at Shawbridge, Quebec, around 1932, and who now step on and off escalators with the utmost difficulty, were selling ski wear in the ladies' sportswear department, while the young beauties who spent their weekends on slopes were placed in the china department – where "dishes" are supposed to be.

But back to the beautiful blonde suspect. She had a high-living boy friend with little visible means of support, and the two were found to be spending much time and money at such places as race tracks and night clubs.

But if she were, in fact, the culprit, what was her MO, as TV sleuths would say? How was she getting rid of the telltale audit portions of the sales checks that would be balanced by others against her cash at the end of her shift? If she were stopped leaving the cash room, she might be able to explain an unusually large sum of money on her person, but she could not explain away the audit vouchers. With other cashiers nearby and supervisors always hovering around, how was she secreting the currency on her person, and how was she destroying the audit slips?

To find the answers in a way that would not arouse her suspicions, it would be necessary to keep her under constant observation – no easy task as the cash room was long and narrow with little space between the cashiers and the walls. But department store security people must be every bit as ingenious as their predators, and cloak-and-dagger methods were called for.

Change money was delivered to each department not on the tube system before the store opened, and returned to the cash room each night by means of a wheeled cabinet about four feet long, four feet high, and two feet wide. Large front doors locked to protect the pigeon-holed moneybags in transit between the cash room and the departments.

The story was spread that the old cash truck was inadequate and a new one was needed. The new truck closely resembled the old one, except that it did not have pigeon-holes or wheels. The cabinet was moved into the cash room and casually placed directly behind the suspect's station, on the pretext that special heavy-duty castors had not yet arrived for it.

At that time, and for many years after, Simpsons key detective was a tough, rotund, beer-drinking fellow named Johnny Meluck. Johnny believed the only suitable place for shoplifters and other predators of his store was behind bars, but he was not without a measure of sympathy for some of those he would apprehend. Once, when he caught a drunk pocketing a few pairs of socks, he decided a warning would serve the same purpose as imprisonment. After all, the poor fellow only wanted to exchange the stolen goods for a few more beers in the tavern across Mansfield Street. "If you ever set foot in this store again," admonished Johnny, "I'll have you thrown in jail." About an hour later Johnny was surprised and hurt to find the same drunk at the same counter up to the same trick. When Johnny reminded him of the warning he had just given him, the drunk replied, "But mister, I thought I was in Eaton's."

While he may not have been the brightest of store dicks, Johnny must have been among the most patient, for he locked himself in the new cash truck about 6:00 a.m. each day, with appropriate facilities for food and waste, to view the suspect through a tiny hole until she and all the cashiers left after the store closed. Given Johnny's appetite for food and beer, one could not help wondering about the possibility of unexpected sounds and odours emerging from his hiding place. But if this problem did arise, it did not affect the results, for after a few days, Johnny's patience paid off.

During lunch hours, when most cashiers went out to eat, our blonde often worked virtually alone with only a skeleton supervisory staff. When a large sum of cash came down the tube, say in payment for a man's suit, the blonde would return the customer's portion of the sales check and ever so slowly tuck precisely the same amount of money up the sleeve of her dress which had been well-designed for that purpose. She preferred a transaction that involved even dollars, silver being too cumbersome to handle.

Because of the favourable location of his hiding place, Johnny soon spotted her taking money. But cash receipts always balanced, so the audit vouchers seemed to be disappearing into thin air, and it took him some days to discover what she was doing with them.

The vouchers had to be found so that the girl would be unable to satisfactorily explain her possession of them, and a conviction would be assured. Johnny knew that we had gone to court in similar circumstances only to have the judge say, "I don't find it unusual that this wholesome-looking (and put-upon) young lady would have seventy-five dollars tucked up her sleeve. Young women must be careful in Montreal these days!"

Every once in a while Johnny noticed that the blonde kicked off her shoes. This was not unusual in itself, but the way in which she put them back on was strange. Occasionally, she reached down and put her left hand into the left shoe, apparently to pull it on. At other times, she simply worked her foot into the shoe, as she always did with the right shoe. When she reached down to put on her left shoe, she appeared to have nothing in her left hand. What was going on?

Johnny noticed that after she had tucked money up her sleeve, the audit voucher, a piece of light paper about 4" x 3", was left momentarily on top of the desk. The blonde then glanced around the room and placed her left hand over the voucher. With great patience, she carefully crushed it and began to roll it ever so slowly between her thumb and index finger into a pellet about the size of a grain of wheat which could then be dropped into her left shoe where it was not likely to be found and even less likely to be identified. As she started to crumple one of the telltale slips of paper, Johnny apprehended her. She confessed to an amount in the range of $10,000, which by department store rule of thumb meant she actually stole about ten times that figure.

She went to jail. Her boy friend presumably went on to bigger and better blondes. But it is interesting to contemplate what might have happened if the girl had been placed in a more appropriate department, such as brassieres, or maybe in auto accessories – where they do fix flats.

*   *   *

Another insider stole enormous amounts of apparel by a method not uncommon in department stores. But, the unusual means by which she was apprehended, and the extraordinary disposition of the case makes her story worth telling.

In the summer of 1952, our inventory losses in a group of departments which were adjacent to each other – women's sportswear, lingerie, and foundations – were so much higher than normal that store executive meetings discussed little other than who could be responsible and the method being used. Once again it was presumed that our thief had access to many departments.

A. H. Lofft, general manager of the store, had recently hired a buyer for the sportswear department who had come from a department store in Ottawa. On a trip to New York, I found myself on the same plane as this woman and chatted with her for an hour or two. She was bright and knowledgeable, but when I left her I had the nagging feeling that things were not quite right.

A few days later, in September 1952, a group of us were celebrating some occasion at Ruby Foo's Restaurant with our friends and neighbours, Barbara and Tom Harvie. During the evening, Barbara mentioned that she had seen a girl working in Simpsons' sportswear department who resembled a young woman they had known when they lived in Portage la Prairie, Manitoba, when Tom was stationed there with the Air Force during the war. Barbara allowed that it must have been someone else as the girl had not responded to her smile of recognition.

She then began to reminisce about the activities of the girl and her boyfriend. He had been with the Royal Canadian Mounted Police.

"Remember the Christmas Day when the Mountie shocked the villagers by driving a dog team through the streets, mushing and hawing to wake the dead? And wasn't there some scandal? Wasn't the girl accused of stealing from the jewelry store where she worked, to give her Mountie boy friend gifts?"

I could not wait to get to my office in the morning to send for the girl's personnel records. No mention of Portage la Prairie, but she claimed to have worked at a jewelry store in Winnipeg. So, we had our suspect!

Buyers and other employees with management responsibilities were not required to have parcels checked as they entered or left the store, and were usually able to go and come as they pleased. Obvi-

75

ously our suspect was taking advantage of this privilege. She came in very early and stayed late, after most other managers and buyers had left. She also carried a tote bag large enough for a trip to Europe. But, she had to be seen putting merchandise in the bag before she could be picked up; otherwise, the occasion when she was accosted would be the one time that she was "clean," and our cover would be blown.

Johnny Meluck to the rescue again! It was decided that new shelves were needed in the stockroom adjacent to the buyer's office. One new shelf was constructed so that Johnny could recline there unseen from the early hours of the morning until after the store closed.

The first day after the shelves had been installed, the buyer phoned in sick; but Johnny was stuck with his assignment, as he was for many subsequent days, while the suspect was "sick." It seemed certain she had been tipped off, and we were about to abandon our plan and discharge her on some pretext, when she not only returned to work but that very evening, after store closing, loaded her tote bag with lingerie and sportswear. She was charged with theft and jailed.

A search of her apartment revealed a stock of about two thousand dollars in sweaters, blouses, skirts, slips, and other items – about enough merchandise to stock a small store. Which is exactly what it turned out to be! Simpsons' buyer was in competition with Simpsons, and she was stealing to order. Her customers placed their requirements with her and went to her apartment to accept delivery of their orders.

Then the Portage la Prairie girl's story began to unfold. When her Mountie boy friend was transferred to Ottawa, they were married and she secured a position in a department store in that city. Her job there included buying sweaters and, naturally, she met many sweater salesmen. She took up with one of them, left her husband, and moved to Montreal, where Mr. Lofft promptly hired her as a sweater buyer. As so often happens when a senior executive hires someone, the personnel department did a slipshod job of checking her credentials, and her spotty record did not show up until after the damage was done.

Nothing so incenses a department store executive as discovering that a department manager or buyer is a crook. While too much compassion is sometimes shown toward thieving sales clerks, the inclination is to treat buyers as harshly as circumstances permit. So it was that Lofft, on the morning after the girl's apprehension, discussed with me at some length how we could ensure that this buyer received the maximum jail sentence.

That afternoon I noticed a Mountie in Lofft's office. I was not surprised to learn that the Mountie was the girl's husband and had hastened to rescue her from jail as soon as she had called for help. I *was* surprised, however, at the sudden softening of Lofft's attitude. He said. "You know that Mountie was just a hell of a fine fellow."

I was horrified at the prospect of a deal being made to keep her out of jail, and I let Lofft know most emphatically that she had a character about as unsavory as any it had been my misfortune to run into in the department store business. I told Lofft I was against anything except jail.

The Mountie husband proved to be the more persuasive. As I recall, his wife confessed to some two thousand dollars in merchandise – a mere fraction, no doubt, of the actual amount involved. But the Mountie made restitution and that was that.

About ten years later, I checked into a Montreal hotel late one night to find the girl from Portage in charge of a cigar stand. At night, if you please! I could not help wondering how the shortages were going in that small retail business.

*   *   *

The most hilarious sleuthing effort in which I ever became involved did not take place in a store but the story should be told. Why not here?

When I headed the Ration Administration for Manitoba and north-western Ontario during World War II, a black market developed in sugar coupons, which were in great demand by unscrupulous confectionery manufacturers.

The *legal* route of sugar coupons was as follows: they were presented to stores by consumers when they purchased sugar. From stores they flowed to wholesalers, to refiners, and eventually to our Winnipeg office for cancellation. Cancelled coupons were pasted on sheets containing one hundred stamps, and then placed in a large wooden box to await destruction. During office hours, the auditing staff watched this box closely, lunch hours and coffee breaks being so arranged that it was never left unguarded. At night, it was securely padlocked. Twice a week, at regular times, two of the building's porters placed the crate on a dolly, wheeled it to the incinerator, removed the coupons from the box, and burned them in the presence of two ration officers who were required to sign a register logging the destruction.

When the black-market operation was discovered, the Royal Canadian Mounted Police were summoned. Their outside investigations suggested that a leak in security might well be right in our office. Internal inquiries indicated that someone was stealing complete sheets of coupons from the large wooden box. This feat had to be accomplished at night, by someone who had obtained a duplicate key to the padlock.

The night cleaning staff was at once suspect, and many ideas as to how the culprits could be apprehended were discussed with the Mounties. Watching with binoculars from a building across the street, installing hidden cameras, and other such time-honoured devices were considered. All were discarded for one reason or another.

About this time, I started my own spying system that I dubbed "watching the watchers." I set my alarm at home and, when it rang at about 1:30 a.m., I jumped out of bed and rushed down to the office unannounced. And found nothing.

So the Mounties developed yet another scheme to try to catch the coupon thief. One evening I remained in my office well after closing to meet the officer in charge of the investigation. We had decided to spread a special powder on the top sheets of coupons in the big wooden box. When dry, this powder was inert. But, the smallest amount of moisture – even that present on the driest of hands, for example – turned it into a pernicious green dye that could not be washed off. In fact, washing resulted in further impregnation of the skin. Only weeks of wear and tear removed the colouring.

Sprinkling the dye on the sheets would take only seconds; in fact, the Mountie did not even bother to remove his coat when he arrived at the office.

We unlocked the box, and the policeman took from his pocket a small jar with a screw top similar to those used for cosmetics. He removed the lid, took a small camel-hair brush from a special protective holder, and brushed the coupon sheets with the green powder. We then locked the box and prepared to leave. But the black metal top was nowhere to be seen! The jar was on a nearby desk, but no lid.

Now the spartan wartime desks in the huge room were more tables than desks. They had no side drawers – simply long thin legs reaching from desk-top to floor. For security reasons, no papers or paraphernalia of any kind were permitted on desks after hours. Everything was placed in the top centre drawer of each desk.

As we looked for the top, nothing – absolutely nothing – obstructed our view. There were great numbers of empty desk-tops on spindly legs, and a perfectly clean floor. That was all. How the lid could have disappeared was a complete mystery to us. It must have fallen into the crate of coupons! We carefully opened it again, not daring to empty the box because the coated sheets of coupons would have dyed us and everything else in the entire area. I refused to go near the box lest I be caught in my own trap. Using a long ruler, the Mountie cautiously poked at the coupons and shuffled them about. No amount of prudent stirring or prodding revealed the whereabouts of the lid.

By then, the office heat had begun to tell on the winter-coated Mountie. He began to perspire somewhat freely and brushed some of the sweat from his face. In seconds, one side of his face turned emerald green!

Finally, we abandoned our search for the missing lid, sure that the crate of coupons was its only possible hiding place. The lid has never been seen from that day to this.

I was the only person in the office who knew the coupon box contained dye, and I was determined to protect it from all but the pilferers. I had another crate constructed and equipped with a new padlock so that future shipments of cancelled coupons could be stored in it. In the meantime, I left the old box of coupons in the office, postponing a scheduled burning date, hoping the thieves would tamper with it, turn green, and incriminate themselves.

By the second scheduled burning day, no one connected with our office had emerged as a green-stained suspect, and I decided to have the dye-sprinkled coupons destroyed. To protect the porters' hands from the dye, I had purchased two pairs of work gloves which they would wear and then throw into the incinerator on some pretense.

79

Just before the burning was scheduled, I was unexpectedly called to a conference at city hall. As I hurriedly left my office, I gave instructions to one of our employees to postpone the burning of the coupons.

Upon my return from the meeting, I went into the men's room. There, the two porters were trying desperately to wash green dye off their hands. The more they washed, the greener they became. As I left, I heard them complaining bitterly about the green ink coming off the sugar coupons!

The individual with whom I had left the no-burning order had taken a coffee break immediately before the porters arrived to take the box of coupons, and my instructions had been overlooked. In addition, I had contributed to the comedy of errors by replacing the key to the box's padlock on its hook in the security cabinet before going to the meeting.

The black marketeers were never apprehended but, surprisingly, their activities ceased. Perhaps word of Operation Green Dye had been leaked to them!

*   *   *

Once, some years later, my "watching the watchers" system back-fired. When I was general manager of Simpsons' London store, I entered the store in the dead of night and took an elevator to the top floor. I then made a search of each floor, using exit stairways to descend from level to level, until I reached the selling areas and their silent escalators. At the fourth-floor landing, two huge London policemen seized me with what I remember as unnecessary force. Somehow, in my tour, I had managed to trigger a burglar alarm system on the roof. A signal flashed in the central police station allowing the officers to enter the store and investigate.

In the presence of police, I have always felt uncomfortable. My usual fears that I have done something wrong were in this case well-founded: in my haste to catch whoever was doing what, I had forgotten my driver's licence. Frantic (and probably rather garbled) explanations followed. An eternity later I was allowed to return home with a strong suggestion that I leave policing to the police.

The Manufacturers

The department store was a by-product of the industrial revolution, but continued improvement in manufacturing techniques became contingent upon constantly improving methods of retail distribution. Mass production and mass distribution are mutually dependent.

The industrial revolution, which spawned large towns and cities* and the advent of local transportation systems, produced the economic and social atmosphere needed for the development of the department store. In turn, all modern mass merchandising systems had roots in this retailing concept. The department store led to the variety chains (Woolworth's, Kresge's), the specialty chains (Radio Shack, Birk's), the limited service or discount stores (Woolco, K-Mart), and the mail-order houses (Simpsons-Sears, Sears). The mail-order catalogue is simply a department store in book form.

But despite the long historic connection between mass production and mass distribution, the relationship between a healthy retail industry and the economic well-being of the community almost completely escapes the thinking of the average Canadian politician. (Not so in the United States where retail sales are given rightful priority in the scale of economic indicators, and the political system responds accordingly.) Perhaps Canadian politicians do not get enough help from the professional economists, many of whom do

---

* In Canada and the Western United States the factory town was preceded by cities which distributed goods made elsewhere, mostly in England.

not seem to appreciate how the retail industry affects employment.*

Although retailing is one of the few truly competitive businesses remaining in Canada, governments harass it from all sides. When excise taxes are increased, retailers are expected to sell stock on hand at the old prices, but when excise taxes are reduced, they are expected to lower prices immediately of stock on hand. The same thinking is applied to the rise and fall of wholesale prices, where some of this economic nonsense has actually gone so far that legislation prohibiting retailers from raising prices of goods in stock which had increased in price at the wholesale level, was being considered. Of course retailers would be expected to lower prices immediately when wholesale prices went down. In addition, governments have turned retailers into tax collectors by making them responsible for the collection of retail sales taxes, usually with inadequate compensation.

But it is in the field of store-hour legislation that the political mind becomes unfathomable. The inability of some politicians to understand the relationship between an efficient distribution system and total employment, and between retail store hours and the standard of living, is staggering.

In the thinking (the word is used generously) that is done before some provincial governments introduce store-hour legislation, there seems to be little appreciation that retailing and related consumer services, through direct employment, through the factories that produce the merchandise sold, and through the hundreds of organizations providing services (banking, transportation, insurance, communications, computers, engineering services, cleaning supplies, fuel, electrical services, advertising in all its forms) may well provide Canadians with more jobs than any sector of the economy, perhaps

---

* It may not always have been thus. An early history of Toronto contains this statement: . . . "the dry good interest [stores] of Toronto is of such vital importance to the sum total of our commercial wealth, and a factor of such powerful influence in the development and welfare of every other branch of trade as to demand special recognition." Both politicians and economists may have their thinking sharpened by an historic event that took place on Wednesday, January 14, 1976. On that date Eaton's announced the discontinuance of its catalogue business, a Canadian institution since 1874. Nine thousand Eaton employees and untold numbers in plants that printed catalogues and produced Eaton's mail-order merchandise were faced with unemployment.

more than all other industries combined. And this does not include jobs provided in the construction of new stores, shopping centres and downtown developments.* Moreover, as technology improves, primary industries will provide fewer and fewer jobs. Secondary industries, particularly those producing consumer goods, will be expected to take up the slack by employing an increasingly greater proportion of the total work force. These additional jobs will be available only if retailers are permitted to sell the goods so produced.

Moreover, there seems to be a relationship between store hours and the standard of living, with lower living standards associated with areas where store hours are inadequate to meet consumers' needs. Why? Like it or not, our living standards are inextricably linked to material wealth. After homes and cars, most necessities and possessions are purchased at retail stores. Clothing, furniture, housewares, even food, may be needs or luxuries depending upon the financial situation of the purchaser, but each purchase relates to the individual's standard of living. It therefore follows that a consumer's standard of living rises or falls in direct relationship to the comparative value he receives with each particular purchase. The larger the proportion of a consumer's disposable income which must be spent on needs rather than on luxuries, the greater effect purchases in retail stores will have on his standard of living.

If retail distribution is to make a contribution to living standards in keeping with its function in our economic structure, hours in which stores are open must take into consideration the shopping requirements of all the people – not just those who work from nine to five. According to Canada's 1971 census, in 34.1% of those Canadian families in which husband and wife live in the same household, both have jobs. Should such families not be accommodated by store hours? Often the husband and wife have different hours of work. It becomes an economic anomaly to permit manufacturing plants to operate twenty-four hours a day while curtailing the retailers' ability to distribute the products of these plants, and denying workers in such plants the opportunity to make purchases in company with

* The 250-million-dollar Eaton Centre in downtown Toronto is estimated to be providing 18,750 extra jobs during construction, and 10,950 extra jobs in the operation of the store and office complex when the project is completed.

83

their spouses. Husbands and wives, or whole family groups, must often shop together to make the most efficient purchasing decisions. It is possible to do this only when store hours are appropriate for all members of the community. A family purchasing a large item must be given time to move from store to store in a shopping centre, and perhaps from centre to centre, to compare prices and values. There is no other way to obtain optimum value. The costlier the item, the more time required! Purchases made in a hurry often turn out to be completely unsuitable for the use intended; in such cases the family sustains a substantial financial loss as well as a lower living standard. Thus, the intent of the federal government's combines legislation, the purpose of which is to insure that customers obtain the lowest competitive prices, is often nullified by provincial laws governing store hours. Of course, some retailers, believing the lessened competition will be of particular benefit to them, encourage governments to unreasonably limit store hours. Like most special interest groups, their objectives, if achieved, would adversely affect the well-being of the community as a whole.

The general standard of living, moreover, is being continually improved by the daily contacts between retail merchants and manufacturers. The average consumer is not aware of how merchants influence the design and production of the merchandise he or she purchases. Many inventions of new and useful products, and most product innovations, originate with retailers; nearly all corrections to bad design result from department store personnel interpreting to manufacturers the needs and demands of consumers. Retailers, usually department stores, bear the brunt of bad product design, because most consumers complain to them rather than to smaller shops or directly to manufacturers. Some products are so poorly engineered that it is obvious they were never use-tested before their manufacturers placed them on the market.

Although recognized by the manufacturing industry, the problem persists. Carl A. Pollock, honorary chairman of Electrohome Ltd., the TV and sound equipment manufacturer, opened a design lecture held in the fall of 1974 with these remarks:

"We men are most presumptuous in making decisions as to what the women of Canada, or any other country, will wish to buy to add to the home environment they strive to provide. The distaff side has always had much to contribute to the home, school, office, or any environment in which our citizens live or work together."

A reporter covering the lecture added this comment: "Women may be able to tell us more about the state of design and manufacturing in ten minutes than the experts in six hours."

Two memorable items that would have benefitted by female advice come to mind. The first, is an automatic electric iron made by General Electric. Irons with thermostatic heat controls were introduced in the early thirties. In its rush to market a heat-controlled iron, GE merely put the thermostat and control knob on the top of an iron already in production. No one at GE could have tried to iron so much as a handkerchief with the new product.

No housewife could use the iron without burning her knuckles, because there was not enough space between the bottom of the handle and the top of the control knob. Furthermore, the plastic control knob was held in place by a metal bolt that screwed into the metal casing and, as GE's rawest rookie engineer could have told their marketing people, the knob became as hot as the iron itself. The feedback GE received from department stores that had irons returned by irate customers soon resulted in a new GE design. However GE took years to get around to re-designing an electric kettle which was almost sure to burn the user's hand with steam every time the boiling water was poured out.

One of the most outlandish instances of bad design was the first Bissell rug shampooer. It was fitted with a large, translucent plastic tank on which were printed explicit instructions on how to fill it with a detergent mixture and how to apply the mixture to carpeting. The tank had a shampooing tool at the bottom and a handle with a trigger at the top. The instructions read: "Fill with detergent to first line as indicated; add water to second line; pull trigger to release a small amount of detergent foam and gently work foam into the carpet to be cleaned. (But caution!) Under no circumstances pull the trigger too often so that liquid, rather than foam, is dispensed through the cleaning tool. If carpet becomes wet, spots will form on it."

There was only one small problem: the opening at the top of the plastic tank, through which the tank was filled, was closed by pushing on a plastic cap which was supposed to lock in place. The cap was so poorly designed, however, that it was virtually impossible to move the shampooer back and forth without popping the cap off and slurping great gobs of liquid detergent on the carpet – thereby ensuring that the carpet would be spotted instead of cleaned.

Complaints rained on department stores and were passed on to the manufacturer . . . who put a cap on the tank that kept the liquid where it belonged!

Of the thousands of badly designed products to hit retailers' shelves over the years, that great innovation, the car sack, is typical. The car sack was to be a great boon to travellers because the garments packed in it would not crease. But the one sure way to arrive at a destination with a badly creased suit or dress is to use a car sack with handles attached to its ends. With this outrageous design, the bottom of the suit or dress falls in a jumbled heap down into the fold. Car sacks with *one* handle where it belongs – on top of the fold – are great.

Things seemed so bad for a while that I launched a personal campaign to reduce the number of complaints being endured by department stores. In my letters to the heads of offending manufacturing companies, I would suggest a punishment to fit the crime: I suggested to the president of a zipper company that the designer of a particularly inept zipper used on children's snowsuits be made to spend one hour each morning for six weeks unzipping children in a hot schoolroom. This tactic, while therapeutic for me, was an exercise in futility, and my efforts, for the most part, seemed to be falling on deaf ears.

Of course, all bad design does not end up on the shelves of retail stores as anyone who has attempted to pack the luggage compartment of a Lincoln Mark IV well knows. Here, in one of America's most expensive cars, one set of golf clubs renders the balance of the trunk space almost unusable. Then there is the 1970 Buick Skylark which, believe it or not, is so designed that many drivers must undo the seat belt in order to reach the mechanism that turns down the window.

And what about paper towel dispensers in washrooms? With all the innumerable companies making towels and/or dispensers, few seem to have been blessed with a designer who has tried out his version before it was put into production. The towels stick, or can't be seen, or tear in half, or dispensers have silly little levers or handles to turn that allow the water to drip down sleeves while the hand-washer cranks out the towel. And how is it that they are placed so high up on washroom walls that only the Wilt Chamberlains of this world are able to use them without getting their shirt cuffs wet?

My special award in this field, however, goes to none other than the Bell Telephone Company, responsible for hundreds of scientific breakthroughs, and helped put man on the moon. While Bell has been imploring customers to dial carefully to avoid wrong numbers, the standard desktop telephone has been responsible for countless millions of misdialings, by moving about like a ouija board on any smooth surface with every poke of the dialing finger. Getting that finger in the proper hole is, as often as not, pure luck. (Of course, one learns to hold the pesky instrument firmly on the table after a few miscues, especially in hotel rooms at 25¢ a call.) My niece, a young mother, suggests a suitable penalty for the designer. Every night for a month, after waking him from a deep sleep, have him attempt an emergency call with a baby under one arm. Another friend would add that he should be made to carry the baby in his right arm, so that he could find out what it is like for a left-handed person living in a world of right-handed telephones.

The Toronto Star of July 23, 1976, reports an interview with my friend (or perhaps my ex-friend) Robert Scrivener, formerly chief executive officer of Bell Canada. Bob Scrivener has recently taken over as chairman and chief executive officer of Northern Telecom Ltd., the very firm that, under its former name, Northern Electric (Western Electric in the US), manufactured the elusive instrument on my desk. Bob Scrivener begins the interview by stating: "There isn't anything any other manufacturer in the world can do better than we can." May I respectfully suggest to Bob that the desk telephone would be a good place to start. And, I have a further suggestion for Bob's engineer-designers: Go to the nearest toy shop for a supply of suction cups like those used for the business end of children's toy darts. (These cups are probably in excess supply because consumer protection people have restricted their use on toys.) Replace one foot on each desk telephone with a suction cup. But, for goodness sake, don't replace all four, or else the phone may become glued to the desk surface and some nut like me will complain that it cannot be moved at all. Bob, are you listening?

While most modifications in product design stem from retailers relaying consumers' dissatisfactions to manufacturers, some inventions originate in this manner when customers' needs become apparent to stores. This became known as creative merchandising, and such things as the fitted sheet and the electric broom came about in this way.

One foray into creative merchandising gave me some worrisome moments. It also provided an unexpected lesson on truth in advertising. In the mid-fifties, when the flood of textile products from Japan began to cause concern to Canadian manufacturers, but joy to Canadian exporters who found the Japanese in a position to pay for such things as wheat and coal, I suggested that Simpsons should have some bed sheets made in Japan. At the time no wide textile looms were available in that country on which to weave sheets 80" wide, the minimum width for standard 54" double beds. Someone came up with the idea that two 42" strips of fabric could be sewn together and then cut into 100" lengths which when hemmed would provide standard sized sheets, 81" wide by 100" long. Simpsons' linen buyers were not greatly enthusiastic about the plan because of the obvious risk – no one could determine in advance whether customers would buy such an unconventional product. Eventually the skeptics were persuaded that the extraordinarily low price would overcome any initial adverse customer reaction. Percale bed sheets could be sold for $3.98 a pair at a time when the lowest price for the Canadian-made product was in the $8.00 to $9.00 range. Thousands of pairs were ordered for sale in all Simpsons' stores.

I was general manager of Simpsons' Halifax store at that time, but was nevertheless responsible for the entire purchase as I had initiated it through the Halifax linen buyer, a man named Edwards. It was only natural then that I would be concerned when Edwards came to my office and, with a worried look, announced that we were in great trouble with the Japanese bed sheets.

"How can we be in trouble before we have offered them for sale?" I asked. "Our stock has just arrived," replied Edwards, "but the Toronto and Montreal stores received their shipments first, as delivery was made through the port of Vancouver. They have already run promotions with huge newspaper advertisements." Then he added, somewhat diffidently, "It seems that the sales have been disappointing."

As gently as possible he informed me of telephone calls he had received from his counterparts in the Toronto and Montreal stores. The results were not disappointing. They were disastrous! His diffidence was understandable as it was clear that I would be held responsible for the failure.

There is no surer way to give a merchant an attack of department store disease, than to offer him a vision of a warehouse filled with unsaleable merchandise. The spectre of warehouses full of seamed sheets in *all* Simpsons' stores, brought on an attack of gastric indigestion which has never been equalled.

I downed a couple of Bisdol tablets as the prospect of *another* seam fiasco loomed larger. A scene that I had hoped never again to remember flashed into my mind with photographic clarity. Thousands of boxes of women's stockings lined the shelves of all available stock-room space in the hosiery department of Simpsons' Montreal store for months because of another terrific deal I had engineered.

When I was the hosiery buyer in that store shortly after World War II, I visited a rather obscure hosiery plant in Woodstock, Ontario. There I found 60,000 pairs of inexpensive nylon stockings. At that time all better quality stockings were made on flat knitting machines which added or dropped stitches to widen or narrow the stocking to allow for the contours of a woman's leg. The outside edges of the flat fabric thus produced were sewn together to produce what was known as fully fashioned stockings. The seam which ended up at the centre of the back of the leg not only identified the stocking with high quality, but was accepted in fashion circles as having a slimming effect. Thus stockings without seams were for practical purposes, unsaleable. The 60,000 pairs did not have seams. They had been spewed out of circular knitting machines which did not have the capacity to shape the stocking to fit a woman's leg. "But why not put a fake seam down the centre of the back of the stocking?" I suggested. "Then, if the price is right, they will surely sell."

Sixty thousand pair of stockings came out of their boxes. Seams that had no utilitarian purpose whatsoever were sewn in 120,000 stockings which were then placed back in their boxes and shipped to Montreal. The price, proclaimed in full-page newspaper ads, when most fully fashioned nylons were selling at $1.50 or more – three pairs for $1.00. But the mock seam, as it was called, fooled no one and for months while we disposed of them to jobbers and other stores at a substantial loss, the thousands of boxes in the stockroom haunted me. At last when only a few boxes remained I gave them to a charitable organization.

After this unpleasant memory subsided and my stomach had settled down, my thoughts returned to the sheets. I told Edwards that I could not believe that an $8.00 pair of sheets would not sell for under $4.00 simply because of a seam in the middle. I asked him to obtain copies of the advertisements run by Toronto and Montreal. When these arrived we read them and re-read them. A significant fact about the promotion was that few telephone orders had been received. Since the customers had not inspected the sheets, it was a fair assumption that the advertisements themselves might be at fault. It was also logical to assume that if this were the case, the advertisements would have a common denominator that caused the failure. After some study, that common denominator was painfully clear. Someone had decided to explain the centre seam by a phrase that ran something like this: "Re-inforced by a centre seam." Or this: "Durability is increased by a re-inforcing seam down the centre." It seemed obvious that potential customers would be skeptical of a sheet which needed to be re-inforced.

We decided to "tell it like it is." Our copy was along these lines: "It is possible to sell these sheets at this extraordinarily low price because, as the manufacturers did not have 80" wide looms available, two 42" pieces of fabric were sewn together to make full-size 81"x100" sheets. The seam will last as long as the hemmed ends."

The Halifax store not only sold all the sheets it had purchased but also sold the surplus stock of Toronto and Montreal!

*   *   *

Duncan Smith, for many years one of Simpsons' general merchandise managers, now project director merchandise management systems, tells of how creative merchandising resulted in an entirely new manufacturing industry. In the early 1950s when he was the department manager of Simpsons hardware department in Toronto, he was in New York buying and looking for promotional ideas. As he walked by the showrooms of a company which made showcases for stores an idea flashed through his mind. The showcase shelving, which could be raised or lowered by hooking the brackets into slots cut into vertical metal strips, might well be used to provide auxilliary shelves in the thousands of new make-shift apartments being occupied because of the rush of marriages which followed World War II.

He promoted about $1000 worth of vertical strips and brackets in a small advertisement under the banner, "It's new, it's at Simpsons." The advertisement showed how easy it would be for young home-makers to fasten the metal strips to almost any wall with screws, and to hook in brackets at any desired level. Shelves could be cut from plywood or planks. The ad may well have been the most productive ever run by Simpsons. The 4" by 6" space produced $60,000 in sales.

Duncan's shelving was, of course, made for commercial purposes, and had the added disadvantage of import duties. He sought out a maker of drapery hardware who re-designed the uprights and brackets for use in homes and added metal shelves in appropriate widths and lengths. In about the same length of time that it took to install a set of shelves, manufacturers all over Canada and the United States were turning out millions of shelving units and enjoying millions of dollars in annual sales. Duncan sometimes regrets that he did not manufacture the shelving himself.

In the days when I was in daily contact with customers, I, too, had a go at inventing some products. Although most of the items for which I saw need were eventually produced by major manufacturers and found permanent places on retailers' shelves, I had limited financial success on my own. When a royalty cheque at long last came my way for my invention of a bridge table cover with pockets at each of the corners to hold tumblers, I had a photostat of the cheque framed to prove to my friends that I had indeed joined the ranks of the Thomas Edison crowd.

Another Bryant invention – later produced in huge quantities by such manufacturers as General Electric and Electrohome – was never credited to me. It is the ordinary room humidifier.

When I began working in the housewares department of the Hudson's Bay Company in Winnipeg, there was a crying need for an efficient room humidifier. When outside air at below zero temperature is brought into homes heated to seventy degrees or higher, the relative humidity drops to about ten percent. This not only slows treatment of the common cold and is otherwise unhealthy, but the static electricity created in dry homes with wool carpets can cause sparks several inches long as the occupant's hand reaches for a door knob or light switch. The sparks are often painful and frightening.

A humidifier that would conveniently add moisture to the air was clearly a necessity.

Manufacturers produced a constant stream of new models. Some were modifications of old designs. Some used new principles, such as the one with two electrodes, separated by an asbestos wick, which were inserted into a thermos-like container filled with water. When plugged in, the current passed through the wick, causing a blast of steam to emit from a small opening in the lid. The humidifier was inexpensive, relatively silent, and vaporized large amounts of water. It had only one problem: the life of the wick was about one week because, as the water evaporated, the wick became saturated with salts and other impurities. If the owner failed to replace the wick in time, corrosion set in and the electrodes and wick set into an insepar-able mass. This item had a one-hundred-percent return – every single one sold was returned by the purchaser!

I came to the conclusion that a solution could be found in a series of cloth wicks suspended over a copper tank, and I set about to develop a design that would work.

At that time, I lived in a modest Winnipeg apartment with three fellow workers from The Bay.

I acquired a humidifier, discarded by the store because it did not humidify. It was set in a rather large cabinet, but it had a big copper tank and fan. Almost every evening after work, much to the disgust of my friends who preferred to play poker, shoot craps, or show girls the etchings we had affixed to the bedroom ceilings, I brought out the "machine" and went to work.

The problem was keeping the wicks that I had installed wet from top to bottom so maximum evaporation could occur. I tried the tank in every part of the cabinet and used any number of devices to keep the wicks saturated. All failed.

Each night, when I finished experimenting, I carefully emptied the tank, replaced it in the cabinet, and cleaned up. One evening I was surprised to find the tank filled with water. Silently castigating myself for being so careless as to leave it full, I wrestled it out on to the floor, only to find that my friends had filled it with dozens of goldfish!

I donated the fish to the grateful children of reluctant parents who lived nearby. In the process, I consolidated our already dubious rep-utation among our neighbours, including a milkman whose leaving for work often coincided with the departure of our guests.

By the time the fish were disposed of, I had been transferred to Chicago on a special market-research assignment at the recently built Merchandise Mart, and my experimenting came to a temporary halt. While there, I attended an air-conditioning show with Mr. Strass, manager of the Associated Merchandising Corporation office. At one of the exhibits I noticed a small brass piston pump that was used for some obscure purpose, on a large commercial machine. The very thing, I thought! Run the small pump by a pulley from the fan, and pour water – pumped from the tank – over the wicks like a miniature Niagara Falls.

During the trip back to our offices in the Merchandise Mart, I told the manager about my experimenting and how the small brass pump should solve the problem of keeping the wicks wet. He told me that a friend of his in the mart was always on the lookout for ideas that could be translated quickly into new products.

The friend, whom I remember now only as Sam, used the showroom of the Eidinger Brothers on the thirteenth floor of the mart, to sell to the retail trade, on behalf of manufacturers, an odd assortment of items including Eidinger's extensive line of shower curtains but nothing remotely related to a humidifier.

However, at Mr. Strass' suggestion, I told Sam the whole story. I had scarcely finished when he picked up the phone and called a manufacturing associate whose name and company I have long since forgotten. I do, however, remember the conversation. It was succinct and completely one-sided. Sam said, "Abe, send one of your smartest engineers to my office right away. Send him in a taxi." In June 1937, this was class!

A short time later, Sam called my office to inform me that the engineer had arrived. He was young, about my age – and smart.

We talked for a few minutes. He took from his briefcase a few sheets of drafting paper and, in perhaps half an hour, produced a scale design. He left hurriedly, Sam admonishing him to hand-make a prototype immediately, if not sooner.

Two days later, the model was on Sam's showroom floor, working perfectly. The retail price was $9.95! That's right, $9.95 for the metal cabinet, tank, fan, brass pump, wicks, and all.

"We'll have to merchandise this thing as a room cooler at this time of year," said Sam.

"Sam," I pleaded, "this is not a room cooler! It is a humidifier. It just feels cool because of the fan. Even on humid days like this it will add moisture to the air, and, Sam, if there is one thing people in the eastern states do not need more of at this time of year, it is moisture in the air. Sell them as room coolers, and they'll all be returned!"

No amount of persuading could make Sam change his mind. In no time he had a brochure circulating and was filling orders for department stores all over the east and mid-west as fast as the ninety percent humidity would allow. As predicted, most were returned.

But, I returned to Winnipeg with a humidifier that really and truly humidified. After a few months of operation, however, the brass pump became quite noisy. A metronome-like effect was created as the worn connecting rod slammed against the cylinder. As purchasers were driven slightly mad by the noise, they also grew angry with Hudson's Bay Company where they had purchased the humidifier. Returns were, shall we say, frequent.

About that time, the Electrohome Company of Kitchener, Ontario, produced a humidifier with the same basic design except that the wicks were kept wet by a large rubber band which moved in a pulley wheel attached to the fan shaft. The bottom of the rubber band dipped into the water. As it revolved, small cups on the inside surface threw water against the wicks. Not as efficient as a pump perhaps, but certainly quieter! Later I often wondered why I was not imaginative enough to use a plastic impeller-type pump, a feature which, incidentally, would improve many humidifiers on the market today.

Some thirty-five years later, I had lunch with Carl Pollock, founder of Electrohome, and suggested that the design of his original humidifier smacked of effective industrial espionage, inasmuch as it was almost a dead ringer for the one that had been put together in the Merchandise Mart.

Carl laughed.

*   *   *

The fortunes of many manufacturers depend upon their relationships with department stores. Some have enjoyed outstanding success and some have been bankrupted by these associations. The Hathaway story is a good case in point.

About 1952, when David Ogilvy's famous advertising campaign featuring the immaculately shirted man with the eyepatch was putting Hathaway shirts on the backs of thousands of men, the general manager of Simpsons in Montreal was Hartley Lofft. He was a keen merchant, always alert to new products for his store.

Whenever his congenital conservatism permitted, he tried new merchandise on himself. It was, therefore, not surprising that he returned from a New York trip wearing a Hathaway shirt. Like thousands of other new Hathaway customers in that year, Lofft found his shirt to be superbly tailored from an excellent white broadcloth. Moreover, in a day when coloured shirts were unheard of in the best sartorial circles and most men wore white shirts made by Arrow, the soft, handsomely designed Hathaway collar had the priceless quality of distinction that might well appeal to members of the better men's clubs in Montreal.

"Simpsons must," said Lofft, "stock such a shirt." As merchandise manager, it was my responsibility to see that the wishes of my boss were carried out.

At first, sales of Hathaway shirts were rather indifferent because the high import duties increased the retail price in Canada to $6.95 while Arrow shirts were $3.95 and $4.95.

It became obvious to me that Hathaway shirts should be made in Canada for Canadian stores. But who would – or, rather, who could – make them?

Hathaway used single-needle construction, a technique that requires not only unique sewing equipment but also workers with special skills. Such plants were rare in Canada.

Although, as Hathaway's first customer in Canada, Simpsons could become a catalyst between Hathaway and a Canadian manufacturer, we were aware that Ellerton Jetté, Hathaway's owner, would be as particular about management as he would be about the plant itself.

At that time, a small manufacturer in Prescott, Ontario, was turning out a specialized line of women's sportswear. The garments were superbly designed, meticulously tailored, and exclusive enough that the manufacturer could count Bonwit Teller and Lord & Taylor in New York among its customers. Limited quantities of men's sport shirts were also being produced in flannel tartans and fine cotton fabrics – on single-needle machines! The plant was owned by Jim

Walker, a tall, talented extrovert whom I had met once or twice in the course of working with Simpsons buyers in arranging purchases from Jim's firm.

Jim was captivated at the possibility of becoming Hathaway's Canadian manufacturer and I arranged for him to meet the Hathaway people in New York. The preliminary talks went well. Jim made it known that he would not be interested in a royalty proposition whereby he would simply pay Hathaway a flat fee for each shirt produced. He said, however, that he was prepared to allow Hathaway an equity position in his company. And so Jim's Canadian plant began to produce Hathaway shirts.

Mr. Jetté and Jim Walker took an immediate liking to each other and the two became fast friends. Later, when the time came for Jetté to take life somewhat easier, he brought Jim to the United States as vice-president of Hathaway.

Jim continued in that position until Jetté sold Hathaway to a conglomerate, and then moved back to Canada. He bought out Hathaway's interest in the Prescott plant which he continues to operate so successfully that it is always hard-pressed to turn out enough Hathaway shirts to meet Canadian demand.

What did Simpsons obtain from the arrangement? Only Hathaway shirts at the right price, some preference in deliveries, and a relationship over the years that has been more than just a business arrangement.

A small footnote is that my part in this tale almost resulted in ending my career at Simpsons before it really got going. Then, as now, there was a feeling among Simpsons Toronto people that the source of all merchandising wisdom emanated from that city. Except for a brief period in 1961, when I personally had an assignment with Simpsons in Toronto, I always disputed that theory.

Nonetheless, when the Toronto store learned of the Montreal store's success with Hathaway shirts, Toronto management decided to carry them also. True to form, the Toronto buyer took a proprietary interest in Hathaway and was upset that I had negotiated the arrangements. The buyer complained to Allan Burton, then general manager of the Toronto store, of what he considered my interference in one of his special preserves.

At that time I had never met Allan. When I did soon after, he greeted me with, "You are the upstart who is interfering with our merchandising of Hathaway shirts! Don't get involved in any such activities again!"

While my boss, Lofft, was kicking me under the table, I replied that I saw as my responsibility the taking of actions which, in my judgement, would be of greatest benefit to Simpsons Montreal and, until I received other instructions from my superiors, of which he was not one, I would continue to do so. Hathaway was not again a subject of our conversation until 1967, long after Allan *had* become my boss.

One evening during Montreal's Expo '67, I was having dinner with Allan and his wife, Audrey, at the Ritz Carlton. As we finished ordering, a bottle of wine appeared at our table, compliments of Jim Walker who, unnoticed by us, was having dinner with his wife at a nearby table. After the meal they joined us. Over liqueurs, Jim told Allan that he owed me a debt that he could never repay because I was solely responsible for his association with Hathaway.

Allan's only reply was a rather unenthusiastic smile. I refrained from mentioning our earlier altercation which could have kept Jim Walker and Hathaway apart, but when I sent a copy of this story to Jim Walker so that he could verify the facts, his reply included the following paragraph:

"There is a further footnote to the Hathaway story. The same apparel conglomerate that bought out Hathaway in the United States, namely Warnaco, eventually bought my interests in Hathaway Canada and made me president of their Canadian group of companies which I now operate and are shown on the bottom of this letterhead."

The group: Croydon, Don Parker, Hathaway, High Tide, Speedo, Warners, White Stag.

As of January 1, 1977, Jim Walker had taken yet another half-turn around the circle. Having been appointed president and chief executive officer of Warnaco, Inc., the American parent company of Warnaco of Canada Limited, he had moved back to the US.

The Competitors

Until January 14, 1976, that sad day for Canadian retailing, when Eaton's announced that it was closing its catalogue division, every department store in Canada had one principal competitor, and it was always Eaton's.

This retailing giant permeated every nook and cranny of Canada, and until about 1951, held undisputed sway in the Canadian department store field. In that year, Eaton's did about as much business in Canada as all other traditional department stores combined. And, they acted like it!

Whenever it was necessary to discuss a mutual problem – store hours, for example – their approach was very aristocratic. They stated *their* plans, and other stores were expected to follow meekly behind. Some believed that Eaton's carried this attitude even further. William Zeckendorf, the New York developer, in his autobiography, discussing Eaton's real estate activities in Toronto, wrote: "Eaton's is the biggest stumbling block to progress in this city."

It was this condescending attitude that infuriated most of their competitors and many of their suppliers. As Eaton's fortunes declined, however, so did their overbearing posture.

I fought Eaton's all my business life, but their merchandising skills through the years had my unstinting admiration. Even after 1951, when their position began to deteriorate rapidly, I always held that any Canadian retailer who did not consider Eaton's his principle competitor was a fool indeed.

My war with Eaton's began in 1936 when I was research assistant to A. J. Gilbert, merchandise manager of the Hudson's Bay Company in Winnipeg. Gilbert was a superb merchant who had come to The Bay from Eaton's. He imbued in me his violent dislike and his boundless respect for his former employer.

His admiration for Eaton's was so great that he had me prepare for him each morning a typewritten account of what was taking place on all nine floors of their huge Winnipeg store. There was a 10:00 a.m. deadline for my report. To accomplish this daily chore, I went to work at Eaton's when the store opened at 8:30 a.m. rather than wait for the 9:00 a.m. opening of my own store, The Bay.

I quickly developed a work pattern than enabled me to cover the entire store in one-half to three-quarters of an hour. Eaton's occupies a full block fronting on Portage Avenue between Hargrave and Donald Streets. Of the many entrances on three sides of the store, I soon found the entrance on Hargrave nearest Portage the most effective for my purposes.

Once inside the store, I manoeuvred to the head of the line of customers who were waiting for the opening bell in the Hargrave Street aisle. In those days, there were always crowds at Eaton's waiting for the store to open: winter or summer, snow or rain, sale or no sale. The size of the throng varied with the sales promotion effort and the weather, but even during the worst winter blizzards, with little advertising, a fair number of customers turned up.

Since covering the store adequately and quickly depended upon my being first in line, it was necessary for me to estimate the number of customers with whom I would have to contend, and time my arrival accordingly. On the biggest sale days, 8:00 a.m. was none too early.

In addition to the daily reports, Gilbert wanted a barrage of specific pieces of information on Eaton's merchandising and operating activities. These requests had one deadline: immediately, at the latest.

As a consequence I spent as much time in Eaton's as I did in The Bay, and on clear, warm days I was indistinguishable from Eaton's employees. On one occasion Gilbert wanted to know all about Eaton's assortment of carving and kitchen knives and other cutlery items. Every knife, every manufacturer, method of display and other merchandising details must be included in the report. Unlike today's displays, most of the merchandise was in showcases. To avoid spending the entire summer in Eaton's, I made a sketch of the department and began to list necessary details as I peered into the first showcase. One of Eaton's floorwalkers became so incensed that his white boutonniere almost turned red. He ordered me out of the store, accusing me, among other things, of being a spy from Woolworth's. Despite our secondary position in the department store field, Bay people snobbishly regarded ourselves as being at least a cut above Woolworth's. I coldly informed the floorwalker that I was with The Bay, and turned on my heels.

Gilbert, I learned quickly, wanted reports not excuses, so I returned at a time when I felt the floorwalker might be at lunch. No such luck. He rushed toward me shouting so loudly that he attracted the attention of a store executive who happened to be in the vicinity. He pompously explained that I was a spy from The Bay and that he was about to throw me out of the store for the second time that morning. "I work for Mr. Gilbert of The Bay. Do you happen to know him?" I asked the Eaton executive. He replied that he knew him quite well. "Well, he wants to know all about your cutlery department," I went on, "and if you know him, you will also know that he is going to get the information he wants. If I am unable to make the necessary notes I will simply send in people to memorize details and feed them to me out on the street."

The executive turned to the floorwalker and said, "The young man is absolutely right. Leave him alone." With that he summoned the manager of the department and instructed him to give me all the help I required.

The manager got into the spirit of the project and as he took the trays from showcases he gave me a brief, friendly lesson on cutlery. How to buy it, where to buy it, what it would do for the customer. I thanked him, adding jokingly that I hoped that I would not have to suffer any more cutting remarks from the floorwalker!

But the Eaton's executive was not of much help on one of the numerous occasions when The Bay's hardware department was being re-organized. Mr. Gilbert asked me to obtain the name of the manufacturer of a nail dispenser which Eaton's was using. It was a most efficient fixture, shaped like a tree, with a series of shelves which revolved lazy-susan-like around a central axis. Each shelf was divided into bins for the various sizes and types of nails. The bottom shelf had the greatest diameter and was used for the largest nails; the smallest shelf, at the top, dispensed the smallest nails. The trunk of the tree-like mechanism was anchored in a circular cast-iron base.

On first inspection, there seemed to be no indication of a maker's name, but eventually I noted the outline of a metal plate affixed to the base. Although Eaton's was the leading department store in Winnipeg, housekeeping was not one of its virtues. The entire area under the fixture was so covered with dirt, lint, and grease that I could not make out a letter or a number on a name plate on the base, even when I crouched down on my hands and knees.

I went back to my store and returned to Eaton's hardware department armed with a supply of dusters, one of which I had impregnated with kerosene. There, again on my hands and knees, I wiped away the top layer of dirt, polished the brass plate with the kerosene rag, took a notebook out of my pocket, and copied the required information. No one seemed to notice.

The Bay acquired the nail dispenser no doubt at a great expense. It probably did not last long, however, because another re-organization of the hardware department would surely follow. Many North American department stores seem never to have learned how to run a hardware department. Some have given up; others still try. Anyway, today nails are sold in clear plastic packages or tubes – except for the size you want. It is always out of stock!

My most vivid recollection of those days involved a man I often encountered in those early-morning line-ups in Eaton's. Each January and February Eaton's held daily clearance sales of odds and ends, mostly items in broken size and colour ranges, from the huge mail-order plant. Prices were ridiculously low and never failed to attract crowds. Because the merchandise was often marked below wholesale cost, a number of owners of small stores bought from Eaton's on these occasions, rather than from their regular wholesalers. In their determination to pick up bargains, they were often obnoxiously aggressive and, strangely, Eaton's – in a most unmerchant-like manner – aided and abetted their efforts to the detriment of regular customers.

Eaton's attitude at those sales, puzzled me. I could never understand why, when they were so perceptive about the welfare of their customers in most ways, they could allow such deplorable competitors to rush into their store each morning, pushing and shoving and sometimes physically injuring regular customers while stampeding toward the sale tables.

One owner of a small store particularly incensed me. He had flaming red hair and was taller than most of his fellow store-keepers. He was also considerably younger and stronger. Consequently, he was able to pick up the best buys. This man would force his way to the head of the line nearest the sale table which was his target that morning (and which he had carefully reconnoitered the previous evening), run to the table, scoop up in his long arms as much merchandise as he could hold, carry it to a nearby counter where a salesperson would meekly count it and ring up the sale, while the next vulture gobbled up all *he* could cart away. Incredibly, Eaton's permitted this to occur day after painful day, so that by the time the red-headed merchant and his colleagues finished with the merchandise, there was little of value left for the real customers who had braved the Winnipeg winter expecting to save a few pennies – pennies that were hard to come by in those bleak depression years.

Usually on these mornings, the red-headed storekeeper was at the head of the queue at the Portage Avenue entrance nearest Hargrave Street, and I was first in line off Hargrave Street. While awaiting the opening bell, we faced each other a few feet apart. I had adequate time during these waits to nurture my dislike for the fellow.

One morning, as the crowds from both queues merged in the usual stampede, it occurred to me that it would serve him right if one day he was tripped, fell, and missed his bargain for the day. As the weeks passed, that thought kept recurring; however, I was hardly prepared for what did happen. Moreover, I would never admit to being a participant.

But, the fact is that he did trip. Not only did he fall, but he landed head-first against the wrought-iron post that helped fence in a bronze statue of old Timothy Eaton himself. The statue was set against the main bank of elevators, where an Eaton's floorwalker, formally attired in morning suit and white boutonniere, was stationed ready to ring the bell that would start the day's proceedings. Consequently, the fallen shopkeeper landed, unconscious, with a gaping wound in his head, directly at the floorwalker's feet.

The floorwalker must have descended from a long line of English butlers. Unperturbed by the sudden appearance of an injured man out cold, he casually commandeered the nearest elevator, dragged the injured man by his feet into it, and whisked him up and away. It was some weeks before the shopkeeper again appeared at an Eaton's sale. He was wearing a turban-like bandage around his head, and he was considerably less aggressive.

This deviation from good retailing would not have pleased

founder Timothy. Nevertheless, Eaton's pulling power was awesome, and they exploited it to the hilt. Their unwavering adherence to his other policies, in a business that is subject to the daily whims of impulsive executives, was a thing of wonder to any competitors wise enough to take note.

Timothy's principles included a set price policy which put an end to haggling over price; satisfaction guaranteed or your money back (and no fooling); authentic comparative prices; and a sale was a sale (no customer ever found sale merchandise in Eaton's the day after the announced end of the sale).

Eaton's supplemented these retailing fundamentals by such broadly based promotional techniques as "The Store for Young Canada" which locked in the customers from a very early age. At a time when The Bay, for "housekeeping" reasons, was making it quite clear that unaccompanied youngsters were not welcome, Eaton's, on a memorable Birthday Sale day, sold hockey sticks to all kids under twelve for ten cents. Any five-year-old knew they were worth seventy-five cents.

To control the crowds that day, Eaton's set aside one entrance for the exclusive use of their young customers, who were funnelled from the door to an escalator that had no steps, but simply ridges on a continuous belt, and was an antique as early as 1926. From there children were elevated to the fifth floor, much as wheat is taken up to be poured into prairie elevator bins. There, a portion of the cafeteria was roped off, and the line-up was kept single file in a back-and-forth fence arrangement about twenty-five lines wide, ending at the stock of hockey sticks at the cashier's desk. Here the youngsters paid their dimes, went down another old escalator and out to the street, each with a bargain hockey stick printed with the slogan – "Eaton's the Store for Young Canada." Thousands of hockey sticks were sold between the time the store opened at 8:30 a.m. and closed at 5:30 p.m. The line-up of new Eaton's customers never ended – it was there all day!

I remember calculating for my report the number of sales per minute in those nine hours, but the figure is long forgotten. I have estimated, though, that there would have been about fifteen thousand boys in Winnipeg at that time between the ages of five and twelve, and few of these would have been without a new hockey stick that day.

Eaton's success with their "Store for Young Canada" promotions made a lasting impression on me, and years later, in Halifax, I successfully used the techniques that I had learned from Eaton's against them. When Eaton's announced a new store in a shopping centre across from Simpsons, we decided it would be timely, before the construction got underway, to launch a campaign to lock young customers in to Simpsons, as Eaton's had done in Winnipeg. This was to be accomplished by giving values even a six-year-old could understand and by providing fun times children would remember for a long time to come.

It worked. Years later, when I met young people from Halifax, now with families of their own, they reminded me of purchases they had made and prizes they had won – at *their* store, Simpsons. Some even reminded me of a day I would prefer to forget.

In our advertising on one particular "Young Halifax Day," we offered two goldfish for five cents. The manager of the pet department had determined that the best method of packaging them was in small, clear plastic bags. Each bag, containing two goldfish and water, was secured with a rubber band. Bowls were sold separately, also at a bargain price.

To supply the hundreds of young people who had responded to our advertisement, a production line was set up on the third floor so that the children could file in, make their purchases, and march out quickly and, we hoped, proudly.

Things went smoothly for a while, but eventually an excited youngster dropped his plastic bag and it broke! The fish flopped around on the floor amid a swarm of anguished kids. In the growing confusion more children dropped their bags and more goldfish slithered about the feet of the gathering crowd. Children and adults began running to the counter for new plastic bags and bowls, but the fish were too slippery to be recaptured.

Porters tried desperately to mop up water during the unsuccessful rescue operations. Children tripped over mops and fell on the slippery surface, grabbing at lost fish. Soon the turbulence spread through the other levels of the store as still more fish and water fell to the floor. People, young and old, were running in all directions, howling, screaming, and shouting instructions, in a scene that would have done credit to the Marx Brothers. The din became almost unbearable. Within an hour, the entire building was awash; goldfish

105

were flipping around behind counters, under tables, in elevators.

The promotion abandoned, I returned to my office to re-think the whole idea. The goldfish, however, were rather difficult to forget. For days afterward, the dead creatures turned up in the most unexpected places.

In the 1930s, while Eaton's was selling hockey sticks for a dime, The Bay did not entirely neglect the children of Winnipeg. Moppets from some of the more affluent families, who had their hair cut in the Elizabeth Arden Salon, were considered to be preferred customers and were presented with blown-up balloons, that they carried out of the salon on the ends of long sticks.

Even this small condescension to possible future customers did not always run smoothly. As the youngsters marched proudly from the salon down the wide aisle between ladies' shoes and linens, their prizes in hand, disaster might strike at any moment. A ruddy-faced Irish salesman named Burke, whose dislike for children rivalled W. C. Fields', often hid behind a column in the linen department, waiting to ambush the youngsters. Burke had developed an unusual talent; he could flick a straight pin off his thumb with deadly accuracy up to twenty feet.

On quiet days – and there were many – Burke flicked away at every balloon that appeared in the aisle. Whenever there were groups of children, balloons would burst like firecrackers. The victims, howling at the tops of their lungs, returned to the salon for replacements while their parents wondered whether all The Bay's merchandise was of as poor quality as its balloons.

Meantime, on an upper floor, Bay executives pondered other ways to increase sales at Eaton's expense. With Eaton's in such a dominant sales position, it is small wonder that few of the promotional sales schemes dreamed up at these sessions met with favourable response. One, called NCD, for New Customer Drive, was patterned after Franklin Roosevelt's NRA and was about as successful as Gerald Ford's WIN.

Everyone employed at The Bay ran around wearing a NCD button, bolstering the spirits of fellow employees, and being extra courteous to the few customers who showed up, until one day a Bay driver tried to deliver a parcel to the home of one of these new customers. The only occupant of the house at the time was a small boy of perhaps five who had probably recently purchased one of Eaton's seventy-five-cent hockey sticks for a dime. He would not let the driver near the place because, he said coldly, "We only buy from Eaton's." When this story got around the store, the zip went out of the campaign.

Other efforts to make inroads into Eaton's share of the market were equally frustrating for The Bay's Winnipeg management of the 1930s. The big, new Bay store had been opened just before the great depression began. Short-of-cash Winnipeggers preferred Eaton's more accessible location, its huge and complete stocks including a bargain basement overflowing with mail-order closeouts, and its comfortable, lived-in atmosphere, to The Bay's spanking new fixtures, marble floors, and somewhat forbidding orderliness.

The reasons for Eaton's popularity should have been obvious even to the most casual observer of the retail scene. But, The Bay people fell into a trap that has ensnared many merchants over the years. They somehow believed, despite the newness of the store, that even newer fixtures, new decors, and different department locations would make the store so attractive that customers would overlook merchandise deficiencies and other competitive drawbacks. More often than not it was new merchandise and merchandising that was required, not new fixtures.

The Bay's management was, of course, wrong, but they persisted to the point where not only the customers but also the people who worked in the store were confused about department locations. I recall walking through the store one day with a fellow management trainee. A customer inquired as to the location of the art needlework department. My friend turned and pointed to a large, but empty, floor area. Embarrassed, he exploded, "Well, dammit, it was there before I turned around!"

One of The Bay's problems in those years was the result of operating policies designed to please absentee owners in England.

All their sense of autocratic superiority was personified in Sir Ashley Cooper, governor of the company in the 1930s. A man named Warrington, who managed The Bay's office in Montreal told me of meeting Sir Ashley for breakfast one morning at the Windsor Hotel. The Great Man had arrived by ship from England for an inspection of the company's facilities.

Sir Ashley believed that Canadians were still raw colonists, particularly if French Canadian. He pompously gave his order to the

French-Canadian waiter, "A pot of tea. Dry toast, butter on the side. *English* marmalade and two eggs boiled three minutes, you hear, three minutes precisely."

The waiter brought the tea, the toast, the marmalade, and set down a plate on which sat an egg cup with one egg on top. Sir Ashley berated the poor waiter to an extent that Warrington was visibly embarrassed, calling him, among other things, a stupid colonial. The waiter stood silently until there was a pause in the tirade. Then with a white gloved hand he calmly reached over and picked up the egg cup to reveal the other egg being kept warm under its base. He turned and walked away. For Warrington the moment was greater than a raise in pay.

The policies of Sir Ashley and his cronies were administered by bookkeepers and accountants, while on-site merchants often played secondary and frustrating roles. Some operating and merchandising practices quite different from those followed by most other Canadian and US stores likely reduced the effectiveness of their efforts to gain a larger share of the market at Eaton's expense.

The Bay, in order to preclude even a hint of nepotism, had ruled that only one member of a family could be on staff at any given time. In those depression years, that policy made some sense, because it not only guarded against the debilitating effects of corporate incest, but also helped spread available jobs through the community. But the policy was carried to ridiculous extremes. Once, in Winnipeg, when it was found that through a slip-up in the personnel department, two brothers had been working for The Bay for some time, serious consideration was given to asking one to resign. The problem was solved by sending one, a pharmacist, to Saskatoon, and later to Victoria, as manager of these stores' drug departments.

Interestingly, the two brothers were Jimmy and Don Ball. Jimmy, the pharmacist, became internationally known when, running as a member of Canada's 1928 Olympic track team, he looked back, broke stride, and lost the 400-metre race to the American, Ray Barbuti. Had Jimmy won, Canada would have enjoyed a clean sweep in the sprints, for Percy Williams of Vancouver captured the 100- and 200-metre dashes that year. Jimmy's brother Don eventually left The Bay for Simpsons-Sears, where be became the top dress-fabrics merchandiser.

For many years, The Bay had the industry's most enlightened

recruiting methods, and the poorest psychology for retaining recruits. Starting in 1934, The Bay's trainee programme was based on hiring graduates from Canadian universities. Eastern colleges were favoured but a few recruits from Manitoba got in by the back door. They were hired through regular channels, but when found to have university degrees (about as essential at The Bay as knowing the right person at Eaton's) they were pulled out of back rooms as trainees. Two of us who had taken this route – Jack King from an elevator (he got the job because the elevator operator's uniform fit him) and I from a stockroom – were walking across the basement of the Winnipeg store one day with Jack Malcolm, then assistant manager of the men's shoe department. George Klein, general manager of the store (a prince of a fellow, an able administrator, but nevertheless, a former accountant), was accompanying Sir Ashley Cooper on an inspection tour of the store. Mr. Klein stopped and introduced us to the great man as *young men with potential.*

In the course of the introduction, he said he regretted that the company was about to lose Mr. Malcolm who had taken a position with a large shoe manufacturer. Sir Ashley's only comment: "Well, you'll never work for the Hudson's Bay Company again!" While Mr. Klein looked on in embarrassed silence, not another word was said to any of us.

Eventually, we all left the company. Jack King became a vice-president of Texaco Canada Limited and, in 1974, president of the Canadian Chamber of Commerce. Jack Malcolm became president of the Savage Shoe Company. And The Bay became a reservoir of executive talent for other retailers and businesses across Canada.

Many years later, in 1972, Dick Murray, then managing director of the Hudson's Bay Company, called me at my office in Simpsons downtown-Montreal store and asked if he could drop in for a chat.

We had a great promotion on that day, and the store was overflowing with shoppers. On his arrival, Dick remarked that he could never understand how we kept our stores looking so immaculate even on days of such heavy traffic. I replied that it was really no problem because it was a Simpsons tradition. It did not seem appropriate to mention the premise behind the tradition: "Good merchandise displays begin with a clean store and clean merchandise."

Then he revealed the true reason for his visit. "I think it is about time The Bay found out why we have lost so many good men over the years. So, during my travels, wherever possible, I am visiting graduates of The Bay's trainee system who have achieved success with other firms."

In reply, I told him the story of my encounter with Sir Ashley.

Most of The Bay's personnel and operating policies, however, were sound and in keeping with customs of the thirties. It was the hidebound administration of the policies, with the letter of the law taking precedence over either logic or people, that, in the view of many, limited progress.

This sort of rigidity also applied in merchandising. If the hardware department was budgeted to have $50,000 worth of stock, it housed $50,000 worth and not $51,000. All hell broke loose if a manager overbought. But it mattered little if the department had a surplus of saws and no hammers because, thanks to the power of the accounting division, being on budget was the prime objective. This pained A. J. Gilbert, merchandise manager of the Winnipeg store. A true merchant surrounded by bookkeepers, he fought desperately to make merchandising prevail over accounting.

One cold October day when, as Gilbert's research assistant, I discovered that not a single snowsuit was on display in the children's wear department although there were racks of snowsuits in the stockroom, Gilbert was outraged. Rigid accounting had resulted in all the department's snowsuit money being allocated to "Bay Day," the store's famous one-day sale, coming up in a couple of weeks. Gilbert promptly had the Bay Day advertisement pulled and the snowsuits made immediately available to customers who would otherwise have been forced to shop at Eaton's.

Bay merchants had to be extraordinarily tough and strong willed in their constant battles with the store's comptrollers. Perhaps it is significant that two of the best fighters, Gilbert and Norman Douglas, both came from Eaton's and went on to manage The Bay's Vancouver and Calgary stores, reputed to be the chain's best moneymakers during their regimes.

The Bay's operating methods changed slowly. A stroll through any Bay store in the fifties and sixties indicated that the ingrained and rigid policies of the thirties were not about to be abandoned overnight. In 1960, while on an observation tour of department stores in the West, I became the central figure in a situation that should only arise in a merchant's nightmare. In The Bay's Edmonton store I found I was the only living person on the top floor, where furniture was displayed in about an acre of floor space. No salesperson, no porter, no customer was to be seen. Amazed and ill at ease I searched in vain for signs of life. Eventually, a handsome young man in a dark suit with a white boutonniere, obviously one of the current crop of trainees, came out of a far-away perimeter office and, smiling, walked briskly toward me. I was standing beside a rather unusual lawn chair – without a price tag. As I waited expectantly for the man to tell me the price, he hurried onto a nearby down escalator and disappeared, leaving me once again alone on the vast floor. Reluctant to leave even a competitor's store to the zeal of a shoplifter who might stumble into a situation encountered only in his most fanciful dreams, I remained on the floor until another employee turned up.

Downstairs, on the main floor, service was only slightly improved. There I watched a saleswoman, who appeared to be long past retirement age, singlehandedly attempting to serve the many customers of the candy department. That department consisted of a circle of counters and showcases some twenty-five feet in diameter. The centre of the circle was entirely open, leaving the woman free to hobble from side to side and from end to end in a futile attempt to wait on the fifty or more people who had encircled her compound when a sudden rainstorm had made them captive customers.

In another Bay store in the Boulevard Shopping Centre in the east end of Montreal, in the summer of 1966, six years after The Bay had taken it over from Morgan's, the luggage department consisted of one camper's trunk and one suitcase. On them leaned a lonesome bicycle, the total stock in that category. Could the luggage and sports departments have purchased too many briefcases and fishing rods?

But today things have changed and the department stores of Canada are in a new ball game. Merchants seem to be in firm command at the Bay these days. In 1970, three hundred years after receiving its charter, the last vestige of absentee control was removed when the head office was transferred from England to Canada, and the ascension of Donald McGiverin to the post of chief executive officer of The Bay has been followed by some dramatic changes. In Winnipeg, for example, where Eaton's held sway for so many years, The Bay is obviously obtaining its share of the market, perhaps more than its share. In my opinion, it is a better store than Eaton's in many ways. Even more important, in a number of departments it is out-merchandising its historic rival.

While McGiverin bears watching it should also be noted that The Bay's trainee system was by no means a dead loss. It may have been losing top men at what seemed to be an alarming rate, but it was also producing store general managers and some members of the executive team that is now turning it into a most aggressive merchandising organization.

Ron Sheen, vice-president, department stores, and Malcolm MacKenzie, vice-president, personnel, were both trainee classmates of mine, and are key men in The Bay's present thrust up the department store pyramid.

I have a suggestion for The Bay's competitors. It would not be a mistake, as it was in the case of Jimmy Ball, to look over their shoulders at The Bay's progress. If they do not, Eaton's, Simpsons, Simpsons-Sears, and Woodward's may well find one day soon that the oldest company in the business is also the newest leader, for The Bay's retail sales have more than doubled between 1970 and 1975, from $406,096,000 to $892,766,000.

During the years of Eaton's domination of the department store business in Canada, it was difficult to obtain an accurate assessment of its sales volume. Eaton's is a private company and has always gone to great lengths to keep its sales figures absolutely secret. Accurate figures were available to the public only once when the 1934 House of Commons Special Committee on Price Spreads and Mass Buying revealed Eaton's sales from 1907 to 1933. In 1929, sales were $225,000,000, a remarkable 58% of all department store sales, and 7.5% of all retail sales in Canada that year. For many years, an educated guess can be made by using the figures which all stores were required to report to Canada's Dominion Bureau of Statistics (now Statistics Canada). This bureau published total department store sales and also made available a list of the stores reporting. Some, such as Simpsons, were, of course, known to us. Others could be estimated with a fair degree of accuracy. Estimated total sales of all reporting stores other than Eaton's could, therefore, be subtracted from the DBS total to obtain an estimate of Eaton's sales.

Using this method, it would appear that, while Eaton's share of the market dropped slowly over the years, the decline became precipitous after 1951. In that year Eaton's portion of traditional department stores sales appeared to be about fifty percent.

That was, of course, just prior to the entry of the American retail giant, Sears, Roebuck and Co. into the Canadian market through a partnership with Simpsons in Simpsons-Sears, by which Simpsons-Sears took over Simpsons' mail-order business and began operations on January 8, 1953. Eaton's problems, however, were not confined to competition from Simpsons-Sears and other stores.

Many of their troubles stemmed from other causes, some unquestionably of their own making. Complacency brought on by those years of dominance of the Canadian department store industry was likely an important factor. Moreover, it was generally believed by competitors and others close to retailing that certain personnel policies permitted the creation of innumerable small, powerful, hard-to-control empires even at lower management levels. In any event, action ultimately taken by Eaton's management would seem to indicate that there was enough deadwood in the merchandising teams to reduce drastically the company's effectiveness in ever-increasing competitive situations.

By 1960, Eaton's share of department store business in Canada had slipped to about 39%; but it is likely that the dramatic increase in Simpsons and Simpsons-Sears sales between 1951 and 1960, caused Eaton's management most concern. Simpsons, while confining its activities to five Canadian cities, had a sales increase of 54%. Simpsons-Sears, penetrating new territories with new stores, had a whopping 188% increase.* During this same ten-year period, Eaton's sales increase is estimated to be only 37%, scarcely enough to cover the rate of inflation. Moreover, because Simpsons does most of its business in Montreal and Toronto, Eaton's must have been losing ground to Simpsons in these cities at a rather alarming rate.

But other, and perhaps more compelling fears, must have motivated Eaton's executives during this period: succession duties, and estate and inheritance taxes. The principal shareholder, John David Eaton, although only fifty-one years old in 1960, was apparently not in robust health. Selling equity stock in Eaton's would provide a cash fund on which members of the Eaton family, who would inherit

* Based on Simpsons' retail and mail-order sales for 1951 and Simpsons and Simpsons-Sears sales for 1960.

113

the business, could draw for inheritance taxes and other succession levies. Even the Ford motor family of Detroit had adopted this course.

Under these circumstances, it is not surprising that Eaton's top brass became visibly concerned. It is known that they engaged consultants to advise them on various areas of the business; and during the sixties, the first tentative efforts to go to the public with an offering of equity stock were discussed in the board rooms of investment firms.

It appeared that Eaton's was accepting much of the consultants' advice. Personnel changes were frequent and could not be concealed, as a steady stream of ex-Eaton's management people appeared in the employment offices of other department stores. Their merchandising began to put more emphasis on style and quality, less on price. Their advertising changed so dramatically that many old Eaton's customers must have wondered whether their old store had been taken over by a New York carriage-trade shop.

Long-time Eaton's charge-account customers in Ontario became painfully aware of yet another change. Eaton's scarcely needed the services of a consulting firm to advise them to computerize their accounts receivable by 1964. Despite the problems that charge-account holders were having in getting used to the computers, department stores throughout North America were discovering that computerized accounting is a vital tool in the battle for financial survival. But the method Eaton's (or their consultants) dreamed up to convert to the computer resulted in a breakdown in the billing system so massive that almost every Eaton's account holder in Ontario suffered. Many who found it impossible to get their accounts straightened out lost patience, closed their accounts, and patronized other stores.

The principal beneficiaries of this fiasco were Simpsons in Toronto and London, and Simpsons-Sears elsewhere in Ontario. A steady stream of former Eaton's customers marched across Queen Street in Toronto and down King Street in London, to become new charge-account customers at Simpsons. The transfer of sales volume from Eaton's to other stores is, of course, incalculable, but it must have been in the millions. More important, the disaster struck at a time when Simpsons and Simpsons-Sears, having broken Eaton's stranglehold on the Ontario department store business, were ready and waiting to make the most of this windfall.

Eaton's people, understandably, have been reluctant to talk about their computer problems. Information has been gathered from outside computer experts and credit executives, whose business it was to analyze Eaton's difficulties in order to avoid incurring similar problems in their own operations. Apparently, Eaton's charge-account problems stemmed from three sources:

1. Conversion to the computer was made overnight for every one of Eaton's Ontario account customers, perhaps half a million in all.
2. Every customer was assigned a new account number.
3. The change was made from what is known as "country club" billing to "descriptive" billing.

Overnight conversion was likely the culprit which caused the most damage. Every Eaton's account customer became involved at the same instant, and the sheer volume of enquiries and, later, complaints was apparently too much for any credit department to cope with, no matter how efficient the operation might be.

The confusion at Eaton's was compounded because the system used to inform purchasers of the items for which they were being billed was also changed. Like most other stores, Eaton's had been sending to customers with their statements the actual bills made out at the time of purchase. This system is known as "country club" billing, because it had been in widespread use for many years at golf clubs and the like, where all chits signed by members are returned to them after their accounts are paid. Eaton's changed to "descriptive" billing, which lists on the statement the date of purchase and a short description of the merchandise. This method has the advantage of making the envelope received by the customer a little less bulky, but that is about all.

It would seem that Eaton's trouble began the first day under the new system. Every Eaton's customer had a new account number, so that the credit department staff was called upon immediately to answer a great number of enquiries as to why numbers held by customers for years had been changed. Many thought their credit ratings had been downgraded, because the new numbers were so much higher than the old. As all accounts were centralized in Toronto, customers in other cities had no one to ask. They could only relay enquiries and complaints to Toronto and hope for the best.

But the stream of enquiries about numbers turned into a flood of complaints as customers began receiving their statements. Overnight introduction of the new system resulted in delays in mailing statements to customers and many were as much as a month or two late. When the statements did arrive they did not include the bill for each purchase, which account-holders had used for years to check the amounts owing. Instead, the statement contained a brief description of purchases and dates:

2/7/74   toiletries   8.37

Previously, the entire bill would have accompanied the statement, providing all details:

2/7/74   Dept. 21

1 E. A. bath soap	3.50
2 Crest toothpaste@1.09	2.18
1 Milk plus 6	2.29
	7.97
Tax	.40
	8.37

Customers found it impossible to remember the details of a purchase such as drug sundries, made two months previously. When enquiries or complaints were not resolved quickly, new complaints were lodged, sometimes three or four complaints related to the same item.

Soon Eaton's staff was unable to handle the masses of work. Billings were delayed further, with each delay resulting in a new batch of complaints. The snowballing effect was enormous. Some customers did not receive any statement for months; a great proportion of Eaton's account-holders simply had no idea how much they owed and, as any good retailer will tell you, when a charge-account customer does not know how much he owes a store, he stops buying from that store.

The charge-account fiasco was prolonged by another management decision. At the start, NCR equipment had been used but, gradually, as things went from bad to awful, Eaton's became disenchanted with NCR. Then, as baseball clubs change managers during a losing streak, Eaton's changed to IBM.

An outsider would have difficulty judging if or how fast this change enabled Eaton's to bring the situation under control. Indeed, it might be difficult for Eaton's people themselves to determine whether a cure had been hastened. One thing seems certain: the change to new equipment resulted in more billing delays and more complaints, before things returned to normal.

The charge-account nightmare may well be forgotten by Eaton's current management, and by the hundreds of thousands of customers who remained with Eaton's through thick and thin. It is, however, fondly remembered by Simpsons – and its other beneficiaries.

To most observers of Eaton's, the climax of their reorganization plans came with the appointment of a non-Eaton, R. J. Butler, as president of the operating company, the T. Eaton Co., Ltd. Between 1964, when rumours of Eaton's plans to sell equity stock began to surface, and the date of Mr. Butler's appointment in 1969, stories of Eaton's efforts to present an acceptable prospectus to the public indicated almost frantic attempts to improve balance sheets and earnings reports. Many of the rumoured changes, such as a proposed link-up with J. C. Penney, the United States' second largest retail mail-order chain, have become common knowledge. By 1970, Eaton's executives were openly talking of going public. So, it seems safe to assume that many of the rumours of their financial problems are true. One thing seems sure. If all the facts were made available, the case history would be a classic for the Harvard School of Business. And, if minutes of Eaton's board meetings were made available, the *New Yorker* could publish under its "Annals of Business" banner an article of the calibre of their superb 1959 series on the birth and death of the Edsel automobile.

Two moves made by Eaton's in the late sixties and early seventies, apparently designed to produce a track record in profits acceptable to the financial community, must have seemed strange to security analysts: the appointment of Butler as president and chief executive officer, and Eaton's experiment with Horizon stores.

Mr. Butler's appointment in 1969 was extraordinary. Just eight years earlier, he had held the relatively unimportant post of assistant manager of Eaton's then-new London, Ontario store. His meteoric rise in corporate ranks surprised both outsiders and Eaton's executives. Butler was not only the first non-Eaton to hold the top job, but also he jumped over a senior and experienced merchandiser, Donald

McGiverin, to get it. Shortly thereafter, Mr. McGiverin moved over to Eaton's arch-rival in Western Canada, the Hudson's Bay Company. McGiverin's progress with The Bay matched Butler's with Eaton's. In less than four years, he became president of the company and one of the most powerful men in the department store field in Canada. He appears to be using that power to make gains for The Bay at the expense of his former employers.

The Horizon stores experiment, Eaton's second strange decision, was well-named. It began when trouble loomed on the horizon for exactly this type of limited-service or discount store. Sayvette, Towers, and Miracle Mart were obviously having profit problems in Canada, Korvettes and others in the United States. The timing of the Horizon move seemed inappropriate for another reason. Most observers believed Eaton's should be concentrating on updating and adding to their existing conventional department store facilities to catch up with Simpsons-Sears and Simpsons, The Bay, and Woodward's.

Eaton's-watchers had yet another surprise in March of 1975, when R. J. Butler was made chairman and Earl Orser was appointed president and chief executive officer. Mr. Orser was not only another non-Eaton, but had no merchandising experience of any kind. In fact, he had joined Eaton's as a financial vice-president just two years earlier. Orser came to Eaton's from being vice-president, finance, at Air Canada (where the quality of customer service had been deteriorating for years). It seemed inconceivable that a financial man, with no merchandising experience, was given the task of running a huge retail business that depends on merchandise and service. Meanwhile, Mr. Butler,* the merchant, according to the appointment announcement, assumed responsibility for a function usually associated with finance: long-range planning. Curiouser and curiouser, as Alice would say.

And Alice may have been right. There is a curious irony to these top-management changes at The Bay and Eaton's. In the days when

* In January 1977, Mr. Butler forestalled further exposure to department store disease by leaving Eaton's. He was appointed Ontario's Deputy Minister of Consumer and Commercial Relations. As far as I know, stomach ulcers are not an occupational hazard of the civil servant.

The Bay found it most difficult to cope with Eaton's competition, the company was accused of being run by bookkeepers rather than merchants. Now the shoe is on the other foot. It is Eaton's that is being guided by the accounting mind, and The Bay has an established merchant at the helm.

The financial man, Mr. Orser, did not take long to put his accounting mind to work. The result provided the retail industry in Canada with its greatest shock in history. Stock brokers and bankers in posh executive suites, and farmers in the remote areas of the prairies, were stunned by Eaton's announcement of January 14, 1976, that their famed catalogue would be discontinued and catalogue operations wound up. The news that Eaton's would no longer solicit orders by mail, a practice founder Timothy began in 1874, and would issue no more catalogues, a Canadian institution since its inception in 1884, was given ample coverage in the Nation's press. The *Financial Post* and the *Globe and Mail* covered the business and financial community with stories of the $17,000,000 loss Eaton's catalogue operations sustained in 1974, and speculation as to why Eaton's had failed in a field where others were prospering. The *Winnipeg Free Press* covered the farmers with a cartoon that summed it all up. It showed an outhouse on the prairie, typical of those where Eaton's catalogues had served a utilitarian as well as an entertainment purpose for almost one hundred years. The caption was provided by a voice emanating from within: "Better renew that Free Press subscription, Ma. We ain't gonna get Eaton's catalogues no more."

The loss to the farmers and other consumers, both practical and psychological, will no doubt be quickly replaced by Simpsons-Sears mail-order facilities and catalogues. Losses in sales and profits to Eaton's suppliers and their catalogue printer, Southam-Murray, and the loss of employment in these firms, will be recovered slowly. Some jobs and profits are unquestionably gone forever.

This latest chapter in Eaton's history is by far the most surprising and dramatic. When I began to write this book in the fall of 1974, I felt I had many interesting and informative things to relate about Eaton's. My first draft of the Eaton's story would permit me to claim to be somewhat of a prophet, although an unhappy one. But, it is unlikely that the most omniscient of soothsayers could have foreseen, or received any pleasure from, Eaton's giving up a century-old business with more than $300,000,000 in annual sales.

Why? The financial pages have printed column after column of comments and analyses, and security analysts have been hard at work assessing the effects Eaton's beneficence will have on the sales and profits of Simpsons-Sears, Simpsons, and other retailers. The most astute students of the retail industry, highly placed department store executives, and top-notch security analysts, would have to go along with the analyses that appeared in such publications as the *Financial Post* and the *Globe and Mail's* Report on Business. In general these reports place the blame for Eaton's failure on one major factor: merchandise carried by the mail-order division and shown in catalogues was, except for a 15% overlap in some hard lines and staples, entirely different from merchandise carried in the stores. About 65% of catalogue and store merchandise is identical at Simpsons-Sears.

Eaton's policy had obvious built-in inefficiencies. Two completely different buying organizations were required. Two teams of buyers had to be paid, and two sets of offices provided. The two separate inventories required for the stores and the catalogue substantially increased expenses. Interest charges to cover the two investments in merchandise would be substantially higher, and warehouse space and warehousing personnel requirements greater than necessary. Further, by reducing the number of items which could be purchased in quantity, different stocks for catalogue and stores resulted in higher merchandise costs.

Other problems said to be contributing to Eaton's financial difficulties were the company's inability to innovate, and inferior market penetration with order offices in 150 fewer communities than Simpsons-Sears. But these very valid conclusions barely scratch the surface of the cause of the decline in Eaton's mail-order fortunes which began when Sears, Roebuck joined forces with Simpsons in 1953 to form Simpsons-Sears.

At that time Eaton's was much more powerful in Canada than Sears was in the United States – a fact that was not appreciated by some of Sears top executives, who thought Eaton's would turn over and drop dead as soon as Sears showed up.*

* In 1952, Eaton's sales must have been over $500,000,000 – equivalent to 5 billion dollars in the United States where, with a population ten times that of Canada's, Sears sales were only $2,657,408,447. The 1934 Special Committee of the House of Commons on Price Spreads and

But this very dominance may have started Eaton's on the downhill course. In 1953, Simpsons-Sears undertook to change the established practice of including in the retail price all delivery charges for items shown in catalogues. Catalogue prices were reduced and freight or express charges for all "heavy goods" (refrigerators, washing machines, lawn mowers, and the like) were to be paid by the customer. This was the highly successful mail-order method used by Sears in the US. Eaton's was expected to adopt the system after one or two seasons of competition against Simpsons-Sears lower catalogue prices. But Eaton's did not go along, and it soon turned out that the Canadian customer – as the Sears people from Chicago were to learn slowly, and sometimes painfully, over the years – was a vastly different kind of person than his US counterpart. Years of struggling with a climate less conducive to shopping by automobile, a higher percentage of the population out of range of centres with adequate retail facilities, and a lower standard of living had produced a much more sophisticated and knowledgeable consumer in Canada than those who were Sears customers in the US, and there were more Eaton believers than Simpsons-Sears believers around in those days. Customers took a quick look at Simpsons-Sears prices, added delivery charges, decided the savings were nebulous to say the least, and transferred their business to Eaton's. Moreover, many customers believed Simpsons-Sears were charging for delivery of *all* catalogue merchandise, so the change adversely affected Simpsons-Sears sales in "soft lines" as well. Simpsons-Sears catalogue sales, expected to increase sharply in response to the Sears magic touch, instead went all to hell, and after a few boardroom squabbles, Simpsons directors prevailed over Sears, and the company reverted to including delivery charges in the pricing of catalogue items.

This initial defeat of Simpsons-Sears was pretty heady stuff for Eaton's. But the winning of this and many other battles in the early years of competition probably cost Eaton's the war. For this was the first of many mistakes to be made by Eaton's management.

You see, Simpsons-Sears was right about making the customer

Mass Buying states that, relatively, Eaton's was the largest department-store chain/mail-order house in the world, doing 7.5% of total retail sales in Canada in 1929 compared to Sears, Roebuck's 0.9%.

responsible for shipping charges*, and any management of that day with reasonable foresight, the essential element of good planning, could have anticipated sharp increases in freight, express, and postal rates. The added flexibility in profit management provided to a mail-order house by charging shipping costs to the customer should have been obvious. Moreover, Sears success with this system in the US should have provided Eaton's decision-makers with some guidance.

But this judgement may be too harsh. To expect Eaton's executives in 1953 to look ahead to 1973 is somewhat unfair. But to fail to understand, or understanding, fail to take appropriate action to avoid foundering when the Eaton mail-order ship began running into heavy seas, boggles the imagination. There is an old axiom in the retail business which goes like this:

> "Any idea that works is a good idea, no matter who thinks of it first. Don't be too proud (or stubborn) to use the successful ideas and methods of others."

Some reports have accused Eaton's of being copiers rather than innovators. If this is an accurate judgement, why in the name of the heavenly overseer of retailing would they not have copied in this vital area, where the remarkable successes of others in the field were so plainly to be seen? Sears-Roebuck, Simpsons-Sears, and J. C. Penney could all be used as models. J. C. Penney, the company with which Eaton's negotiated for over two years, issued its very first catalogue less than ten years before talks with Eaton's began. It was a success from the start. It is an intriguing question not answered, in my opinion, by all the words that have so far been written on the subject.

Two factors appear to have been overlooked in the financial columns. When identical items are sold in catalogues and stores, the two divisions become mutually supporting. The catalogue acts as a sales promotion medium for the stores and the stores act as a showroom for the catalogue. Customers have available to them in the large seasonal books an assortment of merchandise beyond the physical capacity of any store to stock. But the key styles and quali-

* In January 1977, Eaton's Toronto began charging fifty cents for delivering merchandise with a value of less than ten dollars ordered from their *retail* store.

ties in almost every line are on display and on sale at higher than catalogue prices in the stores. Once attracted to the store by the catalogue, the customer has the choice of taking the item home at once at a higher price or walking to a nearby order desk, placing an order, and waiting a week or two for delivery. If the item is not carried by the store, the mail order gets the business. In Simpsons-Sears, the company is competing with itself; but the store manager does not mind because he gets credit for sales made in his store by the catalogue. In contrast, Eaton's two buying teams, one for mail order, one for stores, could not help competing with each other. And, like competition which often develops between branches of the same family* the rivalry can become bitter and destructive. The two buying organizations of Eaton's may well have been more antagonistic toward each other than to Simpsons or Simpsons-Sears.

The second factor being overlooked, or at least not being discussed, is this: In a newspaper interview, announcing the end of the catalogues, Orser admitted that merchandise carried in retail stores and shown in catalogues should be largely identical. But surely this was known long ago. The evidence supporting this method of operation is overwhelming. Then knowing, why was appropriate action not taken? The answer must be that a bureaucracy had developed in Eaton's separate buying organizations, about as rigid as those found in most governments, which Eaton's top management was unable to change. No other analysis of the problem seems to fit. While it is understandable that an entrenched bureaucratic system would evolve (Eaton's had used separate mail-order and retail store buyers for fifty years or more), the inability of Eaton's management to cope is more difficult to comprehend. After all, the organization had taken vigorous, perhaps ruthless, action to correct some of its other problems. It would seem fair to conclude that the failure of Eaton's management to deal with the intransigence of their buying organizations would be as much to blame for their catalogue troubles as bad judgement.

The Horizon Store decision, however, may have been bad judgement, pure and simple. It is now generally agreed that this project

* The animosity between two branches of a family, one of which makes Adidas, the other Puma athletic shoes, was highlighted during the 1976 Olympic games, when some efforts by the two companies to use athletes to promote their products were questioned.

may well be in trouble. Not only was the move to set up the discount store division untimely in itself, but, incredibly, Eaton's did not duplicate catalogue stocks in these stores either. A third expensive – and unnecessary – buying organization was set up!

So, the final chapter is yet to be written. Eaton's remains a private company, one of the largest in the world, despite the loss of the catalogue business. Mr. Orser, when he took over, said there were no "imminent" plans to offer equity shares to the public. But this should not surprise security analysts. They often relate the strength of a company to its depth of management. A huge firm which issues no financial reports, and has a chief executive officer only two years with the company, may well find the investment community in a skeptical mood.

But let us hope that a turning point has been reached, and the worst is past. Because, in Canada's first century, Eaton's contributed more to the nation's growth than any other retail organization. Canada needed a powerful Eaton's in the past and it will need one in the future, because a healthy economy depends on a healthy competitive retail industry, no matter what some politicians may think. And Eaton's always was the supreme competitor. A revived Eaton's will contribute as much to Canada's growth in the next hundred years as it did in the first.

In the meantime, however, the fact must be faced that Eaton's *has* lost its position as Canada's largest department store chain. Estimated sales for 1975 are $1,400,000,000.* Simpsons-Sears had sales of $1,548,600,000; Simpsons, $547,939,763. And the combination of Simpsons-Sears and Simpsons, which began with $200,000,000 in sales in 1952, had increased sales by over ten times to a whopping $2,096,539,763 in 1975.

* including $300,000,000 in mail-order sales, most of which will be lost in 1976 and in future years.

124

The Characters

Some people are just not temperamentally suited to working in department stores. Nevertheless, they are employed by them. This was especially true during the depression years when any job was difficult to find.

One such miscast person was my friend Harry Junkin. In later life Harry became a famous television writer and producer in Canada, the United States, and England, and his quick wit was legendary. (When asked at a Royal Canadian Air Force induction interview whether he was mechanically inclined, he replied, "Hell no. It is only with the utmost difficulty that I can flush a toilet.") Eventually Harry moved on to London, England. His name last came to my attention on a TV screen in connection with "The Saint" series. But on the day during the thirties when Harry left the employ of the Hudson's Bay Company, he was a clerk in the ladies' shoe department of the Winnipeg store, and clearly not cut out for the job.

While Harry sold shoes, I was assistant manager of the fabric department, which was across the main aisle from Harry's department. Early one afternoon, I heard a commotion in the shoe department and walked across the aisle to see what was going on.

A rather large woman was standing up in front of a fitting chair, shouting at the top of her voice. Surrounding her, on the floor, were many pairs of shoes arranged in a semi-circle. Against a nearby column leaned Harry, with a malicious, self-satisfied grin on his face.

Harry, the woman said, had just told her that there was simply nothing in The Bay's stock that would fit her and that she should be wearing horseshoes since she was nothing but a horse and a fat one at that. I looked questioningly at Harry, hoping he would assure me that she had misunderstood him. Instead he calmly repeated that the customer was nothing but a big, fat horse and said that a more appropriate place for her to look for shoes would be in a blacksmith's shop where there would be some hope of her being fitted.

As I gazed at the shoes on the floor around the customer, I understood what had happened. I also desperately wanted to laugh. I was able to control the temptation only because I knew that Harry was likely to be fired and, if I laughed rather than intervene on the customer's behalf, I would be fired too. I was, therefore grateful to be rescued from further involvement by the appearance of Doug Beattie, the ladies' shoe department manager, and retreated to the safety of silks and laces.

What had happened, as Harry later confirmed, was simple enough. There was a strict rule in the department that no more than five pairs of shoes could be shown to a customer at one time. The reason was obvious: to prevent loss of sales because other salespeople assumed that the sizes, widths, and colours not in the stockroom had been sold. Harry's customer, however, would not allow any of the shoes he had shown her to be returned to the stockroom. As the circle of shoes on the floor expanded, he became apprehensive that the manager might find that he had once again violated the five-pair rule. Eventually, Harry concluded that the jig was up and, since he would more than likely be fired anyway, he might as well let his customer know what he had had on his mind as he trudged back and forth to the stockroom searching in vain for shoes that would both fit and please her.

The private secretary of the store superintendent who gave Harry his exit interview told me that Harry came out of the superintendent's office, walked pensively down a long corridor, turned around, and walked back to the door he had just closed. He re-opened the door and called in to the superintendent, "I still think she should be wearing horseshoes!"

* * *

Not all salespeople who find the department store business incompatible suffer from Harry's lack of interest in his work. Sometimes overenthusiasm can cause almost as much trouble. One salesman had to leave the business because his zealous selling inevitably resulted in *some* problem even in the simplest of transactions. He was

Jimmy Smith, and he worked for Simpsons in Montreal in the 1950s.

On a summer morning when I was merchandise manager of the Montreal store, I received a phone call from a customer who was at the United States customs office at Rouse's Point, New York. He told me that one of our salesmen in the luggage department was causing him great inconvenience and, further, had embarrassed him with United States customs people.

The customer, an American visitor to Canada, had earlier that morning purchased an English leather suitcase in our luggage department, put it in the trunk of his car, and proceeded to the border, about an hour's drive to the south of Montreal. On his arrival there, he declared the suitcase along with other purchases he had made in Canada. The customs official asked him what was in the suitcase. He replied that it was empty and that he had just bought it.

"Better open it anyway," said the customs man.

The customer did and found, to his consternation, a man's suitcoat, neatly placed on a hanger and obviously packed by an expert.

"I thought you said the suitcase was empty!" the customs agent snapped.

The coat, of course, belonged to Jimmy Smith, who had placed it on the hanger during his sales demonstration. After the first embarrassing moments, the customs man and our customer enjoyed a good laugh. Then he telephoned to tell me he was leaving the coat in the customs house and to ask that I make arrangements to have it picked up. He also asked me to suggest that Jimmy be a little less enthusiastic in his sales presentations, because he would have been really annoyed had it been necessary for him to return the coat from his hometown in Maryland.

I arrived in the luggage department about 11:45 a.m. to find Jimmy busily selling suitcases in his shirtsleeves – unthinkable in the department store business in those days. Moreover, he was completely oblivious to the fact that his suitcoat was hanging in the customs office at Rouse's Point.

*　　*　　*

Between World Wars I and II, every department store of any importance in North America had a few buyers who became legends in their own time. These men (the few women in the field at that time managed to keep low profiles) were often European buyers, and their renown in trade circles varied directly as their capacity to consume alcohol, rather than because of the volume of their purchases or the prestige of their employers.

Buyers in any particular category of merchandise visited the same European markets at about the same time each year, regardless of what store they represented, and they all travelled by sea. It is not surprising, therefore, that buyers from rival stores became "travelling buddies," arranging to take the same ships to Europe, stay in the same hotels, and meet as often as itineraries would permit.

One Simpsons buyer had his problems with the bottle, but he was so good at his job that C. L. Burton is reported to have responded to a remark about this buyer's drinking habits by saying that he would "sooner have the merchandise that Gilroy bought when he was drinking than what most other buyers bought when they were sober."

There was little argument in those days that Victor Gilroy was the dean of Canadian ladies' glove and hosiery buyers.

In 1949, when Victor was approaching retirement, he made one last trip to the European markets. At that time, ladies' gloves were one of my buying responsibilities in the Simpsons Montreal store. I had been appointed just before Gilroy's trip began and had never met him or heard about any of his countless escapades. It was customary, however, for Simpsons' Toronto and Montreal buyers to visit important markets together whenever possible. Accordingly I arranged to meet Victor in London so that we could work together.

I first laid eyes on Victor Gilroy when Norman Agar, Simpsons' Toronto handkerchief buyer, and I were on our way to the American Bar in the Grosvenor House in London, after a buying stint in Belfast. I suggested that Victor join us in the bar where we could talk over our proposed trips to Brussels, Paris, and Grenoble. He declined so abruptly that I assumed that I had inadvertently offended him. Perhaps, I thought, he is an abstainer or a prohibitionist.

We chatted for a minute or two until the need for strong drink prevailed – after all, Norman and I had spent a very dull two weeks in Belfast. I repeated my invitation to Victor, pointing out that, since we were about to patronize the bar in any event, it would be somewhat difficult to carry on the conversation unless he joined us. He did.

In the bar, the tension eased somewhat and Victor was, with some difficulty, persuaded to have a Scotch and soda or two.

We had arranged to have Bob Gibson, general manager of Simpsons European operations, pick us up in the bar before going to dinner. As he approached our group, Bob's usually cheerful smile faded. He was angry and, as I was soon to learn, he had every right to be. Making no attempt to conceal his feelings, he rejected our invitation to join us in a drink and insisted that we proceed to dinner at once. Gilroy would not join us, suggesting that he must retire early in preparation for a heavy work schedule on the morrow.

In the taxi on our way to the restaurant, Bob made known the reason for his distress. "Who got Gilroy in that bar?" he demanded. I confessed that I had been responsible.

"Don't you know that when we met Gilroy's boat train, he was in such a bad way he got off the train walking backwards and that it has taken us this last week to get him back into shape?"

Victor had arranged to travel to Europe on the old Queen Elizabeth with his old friend the glove buyer for Eaton's, and a few other cronies. The five-day voyage was more than Victor could take.

The following morning when I arrived at our London office, Victor had sobered up and was hard at work. The office had a number of rooms in which buyers could examine samples, write orders, and negotiate with manufacturers. There was, however, only one room with heat: the long, narrow board room with a long, narrow table. The heat, such as it was, emanated from an electric grate in a fireplace at one end of the room.

Naturally the buyers – unless negotiating with manufacturers – brought their samples to the board room, sat around the table, and worked as best they could while surrounded by other buyers and other samples. On those cold February days, the inconvenience of overcrowded working conditions was almost welcome.

Contrition was not the only reason for Victor's early appearance at the office. He had taken up a position in front of the fireplace, leaning back on the mantel as he inspected samples of ladies' gloves which covered one end of the board room table. Victor had used his status as the senior – and oldest – buyer to insist on having an office staff member write up his orders as he inspected samples and dictated his requirements. Thus, blocking off most of the heat, Victor rested against the mantel and barked out his orders to his assistant, thereby disturbing his fellow buyers who worked at the table in chilly silence.

About noon, Victor suddenly leapt away from the grate with a mighty roar, frantically smacking at burning pantlegs. He slapped in vain, however, for his pantlegs fell off just below the knees, leaving Victor in a pair of grey flannel shorts set off by the long white underwear which had insulated his legs from the heat.

Bob Gibson hastened to the rescue. He wrapped Victor in a Scottish plaid autorobe and whisked him off to the Grosvenor House.

But Victor's problems were just beginning. It seems that his teetotaller wife held a very dim view of his drinking habits. Victor knew there was no way he could convincingly explain to Mrs. Gilroy that he had been working in the board room at the time of the fire. Bob Gibson was sympathetic. Most of the staff at the London office spent the next few days searching the woollen houses for an exact match of the original fabric. Eventually one was found, tailored into trousers, and Victor completed his last buying trip.

*   *   *

Department store old-timers would say, "They don't make characters like Victor anymore." But, then, department stores are characters, too, and they don't make them the same way either. Almost imperceptibly, department stores in North America have undergone radical changes in merchandising and operating policies so that, today, except for some of the old downtown locations, they bear only slight resemblances to their predecessors.

Many of the policies that enabled Marshall Field, John Wanamaker, Timothy Eaton, and Robert Simpson to build great merchandising empires are all but forgotten. Such sacred department store merchandising principles as all departments under one roof, basic stocks, and service based on knowledgeable department managers have been all but discarded by some historic stores.

The department store developed from the logical premise that a store housing all departments, from hardware to lingerie, and from furniture to spools of thread, could serve consumers more efficiently than many small stores spread all over town. What has happened to this concept?

Department stores have for years been discontinuing items, merchandise categories, and sometimes entire departments that have proved to be unprofitable or just plain troublesome. Hardware, housewares, drug sundries, notions, sporting goods, and toys have suffered most. Books, once on the list of problem departments, are now back in the "good books" because they are once again profitable.

The housewares department in many stores is simply a large gift shop, not a housewares department at all. In these stores, you no longer can expect to find a basic assortment of cooking utensils, small electrical appliances, and cutlery. You may well find, however, a vast area housing scallop shells, sea salt grinders, escargot holders, and many attractive but useless gift items from the far corners of the world.

In the summer of 1973, Bloomingdale's in New York had in stock in their huge downtown store, one style of coat hanger. Think of it! The great Bloomingdale's – once the envy of every department store executive with a feeling for basic stocks – with coat hangers in an assortment of one!

And that's not all. The hanger could only be purchased gift-boxed in a set of three. Each hanger was wrapped in satin, presumably to make it appear attractive as a gift, but anyone who received such a present would soon learn that it is about the most inefficient hanger known to man.

This analysis of merchandising trends was written long before *Time* magazine's cover story on Bloomingdale's appeared in December of 1975. Readers of the *Time* article will hardly be surprised that a satin-covered coat hanger was the only style available. Bloomingdale's brag about having dropped cameras, men's razors, washers, dryers, and innumerable other basic items, which they presumably found troublesome or unprofitable. It can get away with this because it is uniquely located, serving an unique clientele, most of whom live in nearby apartments. These customers have little need for many of the discontinued items. It is difficult, however, to believe they are getting along without razors or cameras.

Bloomingdale's has been successful in adapting to the needs of its customers, and has been even more successful in catering to their tastes, but it has ceased to be a department store in the traditional sense. It has abdicated its original concept of all departments from furniture to notions under one roof. Instead, it has become a series of high-class and not so high-class specialty stores in the same building. Mesmerized customers refer to the store as "Bloomies", but "The Bloomingdale Shops" would be a more appropriate name.

If this model is followed by enough others, the department store will have come full circle. It will be replaced by the specialty store from which it sprung, even if all its specialty stores are in one building.

It must be said, however, that Bloomingdale's is the most talked-about store in North America, if not the best. There would not be sufficient funds in all the advertising budgets of all US stores combined to buy the publicity created by the *Time* magazine story. *Time's* article was only the beginning. About every newspaper and magazine in the US, and many the world over, picked up the theme and filled columns and pages extolling Bloomingdale's. There is little doubt that Queen Elizabeth's visit to the store on Saturday, July 10, 1976, was a result of this widespread publicity. According to newspaper stories, Prince Philip was shown some of Bloomingdale's best sellers. One of these was the famed Pet Rock. This bit of merchandising hokum consisted of an ordinary rock, cleverly packaged, with tongue-in-cheek instructions like – "to make the rock come to you, hold it on sloping surface, yell 'come', and release your grip." If the Pet Rock, which sold for $4.00 remains a best seller in Bloomingdale's, the awesome power of this gratis publicity is amply demonstrated. For most stores, Pet Rocks have long since hit the markdown tables.* In their place, in the summer of 1976, the "in" item was a can of fresh Vermont air, canned in Massachusetts, because Vermont has no canneries.

Nevertheless, all the free publicity being showered on Bloomingdale's is causing stores all over North America to consider emulating it – taking what has come to be known as the "Bloomingdale route." But, perhaps wise merchants will do what they have always done, meld the best of Bloomingdale's, or any other good store, into their own operations. For them, survival will, as in the past, depend on serving a broad cross-section of customers in the community with a wide assortment of wanted items in medium to moderately high price ranges.

* The Miami *Herald* of October 25, 1976, reported that a Detroit woman had started a cemetery for pet rocks.

A visit to the store in August 1976 would dampen the enthusiasm of the most ardent imitators. Their clock department is, in my opinion, a disgrace to department store merchandising. The Pet Rock, shown to Prince Philip a month earlier as a "best seller" was down to a stock of one, in a beaten-up box, without instructions – they had been lost. It belonged in the Detroit cemetery. (Merchandising idea for Bloomingdale's: buy the surplus boxes in which pet rocks were packaged, and sell them as pet rock coffins.)

Caution is also indicated because, considering the sales of many Canadian department stores operating in much smaller cities, the $160,000,000 in sales attributed to Bloomingdale's in 1975 is not that spectacular. And, if they are offering the same apartment-dweller merchandise to the individual homeowners of White Plains, their branch store operations could be improved, no matter how satisfactory their sales seem to be.

Apart from the "Bloomingdale" trend, what about basic stocks, considered for years to be the very foundation of department store merchandising? If some of today's department store managements understand the meaning of basic stock, their knowledge does not manifest itself in the areas to which customers have access. The chances of finding *your* size in *your* colour are becoming slimmer with each passing year. And, it matters little whether you are looking for clothing, nuts and bolts, sheets and pillow cases, or light bulbs. If you find the liner for the garbage can, the staples for the staple gun, the ribbon for the typewriter, or the brush for your electric toothbrush in the store where you made the original purchase, you are fortunate indeed.

In West Palm Beach, Florida, Burdines does not carry baby cribs or juvenile furniture – incredible in a city claiming to have insufficient school rooms for the growing population. Sears in North Palm Beach, while presenting a January white sale with great advertising ballyhoo, had on display one – that's right, one – quality of bed pillow. It was filled with dacron. No other pillow of any type – feather, down, sponge rubber, not even any other quality of dacron was available on the floor or from the stockroom. And, that is not all! The pillow was only available in one size. The best-selling regular size? No, the poorest-selling queen size!

Department stores are also changing their competitive pricing practices. Slowly but surely, they are giving up the notion that their prices must be as low or lower than nearby competitors. The slogan "Nobody, but Nobody, Undersells Gimbels" was never very accurate. Today, however, it would be a plain and simple untruth, because many identical items are likely to be priced higher in Gimbels than in Macy's – and vice versa.

There is a valid reason for this. The customer is changing as rapidly as the department store itself. Not that he is less concerned about price than he was a few years ago but, to an increasing number of people, time has become as valuable as money. Rather than spend time (and money) driving from one store to another to compare prices, today's customer is more and more inclined to buy immediately he finds the object of his search. With sizes and colours so difficult to find in everything from clothing to bed sheets, the customer is apt to grab the item as soon as he sees it in his size and his colour and think, "To hell with the price!"

In West Palm Beach, an identical bathmat was priced at $12.95 in Jordan Marsh, $14.95 in Burdines, and $8.99 in the Pioneer, a well-known specialty store. A bedspread that cost $42 in Burdines was $36 in the Pioneer down the street. Pricing of women's dresses is surely arbitrary, for differences of $10 to $20 are not uncommon in the $100 price range.

In this respect, the department store is following the lead of the food supermarket which, as almost any housewife will tell you, years ago abandoned the principle that identical items should be identically priced.

Service in almost all stores has suffered, too, for a variety of reasons. Night openings and, in some areas, Sunday openings, have been the principal contributors to the declining standards of service. When stores are open twelve or more hours a day, six or seven days a week, and key personnel, including supervisors, work eight hours a day, five days a week, the logistics involved in keeping knowledgeable persons in each department at all times are overwhelming.

And where would they hire sufficient numbers of trained people? Victor Gilroy graduated from an apprenticeship system which the department store has been forced to abandon in the face of competition from other businesses and industries for the young, the bright, and the educated. The trouble is that no amount of formal training can substitute for time on the selling floor where five years' experience can only be gained in five years.

134

The apprenticeship system did, however, have drawbacks. It made Victor Gilroy a great merchant, but may also have trained him for some of his extra-merchandising activities. Certainly an assistant usually had to wait too many years for major promotion. Usually he had to wait until his boss died or retired. Consequently, by the time he became a department head, he was often too old and too much like his predecessor. New thinking and imagination were stifled.

Deviation from the department store concept is taking place more rapidly in the United States than in Canada. For this reason, most of the examples given have been well-known US stores. Canada, however, is not far behind. Eaton's Toronto has recently announced it will abandon older customers in favour of the twenty-five to forty-five age group.

You may well conclude that my criticisms of department store trends are merely the rantings of a crotchety old merchant who was born forty years too soon. (An idea supported, I suspect, by my son, Terry, himself a "blooming" young merchant.)

But, it would be erroneous to assume that the department store is doomed, or that I believe all the changes have been bad ones. Along with the shortcomings which have evolved, many improvements have taken place.

The fixturing, arrangement of merchandise, and departmental layouts (where the shop concept has not been carried to ridiculous extremes), have all been tremendously, though not sufficiently, improved. Today's customers can more easily inspect a range of merchandise and, as a result, make more intelligent purchasing decisions than did their parents or grandparents. A generation of shoppers conditioned by supermarkets is at ease only in a store where all the merchandise is exposed to close inspection and handling. The demise of the showcase was inevitable and will be welcome.

Suburban branches have taken department store selections to their customers. Although branch stores, usually in shopping centres, rarely have as complete assortments as main downtown stores, they do bring to customers who are unable or prefer not to shop downtown traditionally high department store quality, new styles, consistent values, and generally better service than so-called discount stores.

Moreover, while lack of on-the-job training is a distinct drawback, young people making careers in the department store field today are generally brighter, better educated, and more enthusiastic than their predecessors. They usually learn more quickly and, while a reasonable period of apprenticeship would help, it is obviously not vital.

In the late fifties and early sixties, discount store executives, some economists, professors of retailing, and even some old department store men were predicting that traditional department stores would soon be a thing of the past. What has happened?

The good stores in the United States and Canada – Federated Stores, Allied Stores, Macy's, Marshall Field, Simpsons, the Hudson's Bay Company, and Woodward's, are examples – have continued to grow and prosper and have rewarded investor-shareholders. It is the limited-service stores, the discounters, which have run into trouble.* Many are all but bankrupt – the huge W. T. Grant organization is.

It would seem safe to say that the real department store is here to stay.

* Notable exceptions: KMart, Woolco

The Developers

From its very beginning the department store became deeply involved in the development of downtown (core) areas of North American communities. Large towns and cities had origins in the industrial revolution, which pulled people off farms and out of small villages, concentrating them near their places of employment in factory towns or distribution centres. Cities such as New York, Boston, Montreal, and Toronto grew in the nineteenth century at a spectacular rate. As public transportation improved and the horse-drawn street car gave way to the electric variety, commercial establishments, stores, banks, insurance offices, hotels, and theatres gravitated to city centres or downtown.

The department store, quite naturally, became the focal point of the transition. Larger premises were required, not only to cope with increasing sales volume, but to house under one roof the greater number of merchandise categories that stores found their customers demanding. And, as customers moved, stores moved with them. A continuing search for additional land and/or buildings resulted. Almost every important store in North America found it necessary to make a number of moves. Altman's, Lord and Taylor, Macy's, Morgan's, Eaton's, Simpsons, and Woodward's, all went through a series of relocations and additions which brought them, by the turn of the century, to their present sites.

Thus, department stores, frequently without being aware of it, were among the very first urban real estate developers. And, since stores followed the people from the original areas of settlement around factories, docks, and railway yards to residential areas and eventually to the suburbs, they also became involved in suburban real estate development.

The first moves were "uptown" to one residential district after another, each one further removed from a fast deteriorating "downtown." With each move, the old uptown often became the new downtown. In New York, for example, stores which had opened between 1823 and 1848 moved uptown from the waterfront area at the tip of Manhattan Island. By the 1870s, a number of today's great stores – Altman, Best, Bergdorf Goodman, Lord & Taylor – were concentrated in an area between 14th and 23rd Streets, and Broadway and Sixth Avenue. Early in the 1900s many of these stores settled around 34th Street, where they remain to this day, although a few of the more exclusive stores continued the movement all the way up Fifth Avenue to 59th Street.

In Montreal the Notre Dame – St. James section near the St. Lawrence River was the original "downtown." Morgan's (now The Bay), Murphy's (now Simpsons), and Ogilvy's (still Ogilvy's) all moved to St. Catherine Street from this area. Even in Toronto there was a slight move uptown from Adelaide and King Streets to Queen.*

But even with this tradition of keeping near their customers, few North American stores foresaw clearly the change in shopping habits which would result from the use of the automobile, and from the dramatic movement of people from the inner city to the suburbs.

Oddly, Simpsons had the best opportunity to exploit the trend to the suburban store, because this company developed what was quite possibly the first department store on the perimeter of any North American city. In 1919, to provide better service to the Atlantic provinces a mail-order distribution centre was opened on a railway siding on the outskirts of Halifax, close to that city's famed North West Arm. Discontinued mail-order lines were at first sold to employees then to outside customers through a small retail section in the building. A larger area of the building was converted into a conventional retail store in 1924, from which evolved the present great Halifax store. That Simpsons was placed in the vanguard of the move to the suburbs by accident rather than design may explain why the lead was not followed up.

One retailer who did follow Simpsons lead, probably without

* Eaton's attempt in 1930 to push the centre of retail activity north to College Street was unsuccessful. See the discussion of Eaton's College Street store, p. 19.

knowing it, was General Robert Wood, who headed the huge Sears, Roebuck organization from 1928 to 1955. Under the general's guidance, Sears began locating its stores on the perimeters of cities and large towns. * These stores, within easy driving distance of major residential areas, and featuring plenty of free parking, were the forerunners of today's regional shopping centre, and General Wood is sometimes called the father of the suburban department store.

It was not until after World War II that traditional department stores joined their customers in headlong flight to the suburbs. Moreover, the stores soon realized that while suburban consumers' changing shopping patterns had made their moves to the suburbs imperative, one important habit had not changed at all. The new suburbanites still preferred to shop in areas where clusters of good stores were within easy walking distance of each other.

But even this well-established rule of retailing had to be relearned. It took one or two significant examples, where two shopping centres with only one well-known department store in each ended up separated by a major thoroughfare, to drive the lesson home. One of these situations, in the Crenshaw retail district of Hollywood, California, where busy Santa Barbara Avenue separated centres anchored by the May Company and Broadway Stores, made self-evident to store planners what they should have known from previous experience – that two great stores, both easily accessible on foot, give a centre more pulling power than one.

Later, when the regional shopping centre was well-established, a rather inexact mathematical formula based on geometric progression was used by planners to estimate sales potential. Thus, a centre with two department stores should have, not twice, but four times the pulling power of a centre with only one major store; a centre with three department stores should have nine times the customer appeal.

The shopping centre with a department store at each end and specialty shops in between had its beginnings on the west coast of the United States in the late 1940s. Eastern US stores moved more slowly. Perhaps the first regional centre in the east, Shoppers World near Boston, which was developed by Jordan Marsh and contains a

* Sears first suburban store opened on June 30, 1928, in Aurora, a suburb of Chicago, Illinois.

Sears store, opened in 1951. But some stores, notably Macy's and Gimbels, hesitated. At one point, Gimbels ran advertisements belittling the shopping centre/branch store concept.

If eastern US stores awakened to the trend slowly and hesitatingly, Canadian stores were positively somnolent. Woodward's opened Canada's first shopping centre store at Park Royal North in Vancouver in 1950, and Morgan's opened two shopping centre branches in the Montreal area in the early 1950s, but the first centre with two major stores, Morgan's (now Robinsons) and Simpsons-Sears, did not open until 1954, in Hamilton, Ontario.

But it took the arrival of the limited service or discount store to awaken department stores in some areas such as Toronto. Towers and Sayvettes opened shopping centre stores in Toronto in 1961 with great fanfare. Traditional department stores would soon be a thing of the past, according to many executives of the interlopers. Although there was little chance that this would happen, Eaton's and Simpsons, the sleeping giants, were stirred into action, both opening branch stores in 1962. But it was to be a full ten years after the opening of the Hamilton centre that Canada would have its first truly regional shopping centre. In 1964 Eaton's and Simpsons joined forces in the vast Yorkdale centre in Toronto.

To be sure, the Yorkdale idea was born long before the 1964 opening. Eaton's acquired the Yorkdale property in 1959 with a shopping centre in mind. They invited Simpsons to join them so that the rivalry, which had made Queen and Yonge Streets in downtown Toronto one of the world's great centres of retailing, would come into play at the new shopping centre. But delay after delay postponed the opening. Once when delay problems were being discussed at a Simpsons executive meeting, some wit remarked that at least we would not have to worry about staff for the new operation, because there would be plenty of time to breed them. With so many young, attractive buyers on Simpsons staff at the time, the idea had a favourable reception.

The Yorkdale experience set a pattern for future shopping centre development in which Eaton's or Simpsons were involved. For example, in Montreal, where Simpsons were development partners with the Cadillac Fairview Corporation in shopping centres in Pointe Claire and Ville d'Anjou, Eaton's were invited to become the other department store. At Le Carrefour Laval, where Eaton's was

140

one of the developers, Simpsons received the invitation.

Canadian department stores soon made up for their slow start in suburbia. Between 1964 and 1976, a proliferation of centres took place which resulted in the "overstoring" of many cities. Real estate developers, tossing merchandising considerations and viability criteria to the winds, put up shopping centres in any open space available in Montreal, Toronto, London, and other Canadian cities. It will take years for residential areas to develop around many of them, or for shopping traffic patterns to shift sufficiently to make them profitable. Some will go bankrupt. This trend is less noticeable in the United States, but there is little doubt that entering into shopping centres with marginal locations was a principal cause of the bankruptcy of W. T. Grant and Company, one of the oldest and largest of the US variety chains, and the parent of Zellers in Canada.

With surburbs pretty well taken care of, the shopping centre seems about to complete a giant cycle in Montreal and Toronto, by moving back downtown. Montreal's vast underground city of shops, which began with Place Ville Marie, is being duplicated in Toronto under numerous new office buildings and hotels. In Montreal, a new office building and retail complex attached to Eaton's downtown store presages an eventual link with Simpsons.

Some US cities have joined the trend as part of a redevelopment of core areas, but it is in Toronto that the big action is taking place. There, the enormous Eaton Centre is being built. In true department store tradition, Eaton's is a developing partner. This multi-million-dollar project will move Eaton's store from Queen Street to Dundas and will connect to Simpsons with a galleria housing specialty shops. Simpsons will be linked underground at the subway level, and by a bridge over Queen Street.

It is interesting to speculate what will happen when this giant retail complex settles down to more or less permanent shopping patterns. The rationale is simple enough. The two traditional competitors will have between them the finest array of specialty shops in Canada, perhaps the world. Customers will be lured by a huge new Eaton's store, air-conditioned comfort in the galleria, beauty, plenty of parking, and the subway. Eaton's College Street store customers will transfer to the new location, since that store will be closed. All these factors should be on the plus side. One thing will be lost, however, and there is no way for even the most clairvoyant oracle to predict the results. The missing element in the new arrangement will be the proximity of the two major stores.

Today's customers are attracted to Queen Street, and are willing to put up with long subway rides or expensive parking, because they know that at their destination they will be able to inspect the two largest merchandise assortments in the city, both rapidly and conveniently. What is involved here is the priceless and unpredictable factor of time. It will take just as long as it ever did to get downtown. It is sure to become more costly in the years ahead. The question becomes – will the variety offered by the shops between Eaton's and Simpsons replace the present appeal of proximity? More than that, will the complex attract enough additional customers to pay the rent of the greatly expanded retail areas? Or, will the customers come down a few times, say that it is indeed beautiful but no longer useful (because time no longer permits comparison shopping on one trip), and seek more convenient shops nearer home? And those extra customers that the planners of the centre are counting on, might they not come downtown from their suburban homes once or twice, and then revert to their old habits? Some have not been downtown in years. It will not be easy to change such ingrained shopping habits, as department stores well know from past experience. One thing is sure: the attraction of the centre is unlikely to bring more visitors to Toronto despite developers' expectations. We shall see! If I were still in the business, I would be concerned.

No matter what happens, department stores are likely to have continuing roles in real estate development and will continue to acquire property as the key to future plans. For the assembling of land on which any enterprise, office complex, factory or department store is to be located is the vital first step.

In Montreal, for example, Simpsons always required space to expand the downtown store on St. Catherine Street. From the time in 1905 when the John Murphy Company was acquired, negotiations to purchase adjacent properties for expansion were usually frustratingly slow. Often unconventional methods were, of necessity, employed, and almost always some extraordinary twist occurred before the transaction could be completed.

In his autobiography, *A Sense of Urgency,* C. L. Burton relates how it required some fifteen years of on-and-off negotiations to effect the purchase of a small parcel of land at the corner of Metcalfe and St.

Catherine, on which part of the Montreal store was built in 1930. In Montreal, I was to learn that real estate acquisitions were quite as likely to bring on an attack of department store disease as merchandising or operating problems, as Simpsons attempts to acquire land for further expansion of store facilities and for car parking brought about many unusual real estate deals.

The extraordinary location of Simpsons' Montreal store was unquestionably the key factor in surrounding many of these transactions with an atmosphere of excitement and a cloak-and-dagger quality. The store occupies the southern third of the city block bounded by St. Catherine Street on the south, Boulevard de Maisonneuve on the north, Mansfield Street on the east, and Metcalfe Street on the west. Since the historic Mount Royal Hotel was built across Metcalfe Street around 1920, this block has been at the heart of Montreal's downtown business district. The advent of Montreal's Metro, with its principal terminal two blocks east, at Eaton's, has done little to shift the focal point of the core area, because Place Ville Marie, a mere three hundred feet from Simpsons' main entrance, is, and always will be, the true centre of the city. New buildings springing up all around The Place only tend to enhance its importance.

Between the northern perimeter of Simpsons' store and Boulevard de Maisonneuve there was, until 1974, a motley collection of buildings, anchored on the north-west by Ben's – world famous for smoked meat sandwiches and cherry cokes – and on the north-east corner by a restaurant-hotel, with a huge fish tank in its window, and a bar which enjoyed more localized fame under the name Monsieur Neptune. Ben's was a relatively new brick building, well maintained. Neptune was old and deteriorating, but the owner kept up a facade of respectability with occasional paint jobs. Between these two structures on Mansfield and Metcalfe Streets and Simpsons' back door was a collection of sad and unsightly buildings. The ground floors housed a barber shop, a book store, odd small shops, and a number of restaurants – some good, some poor, and some frightful. The upper floors contained suites or rooms, many rented by young ladies by the month, the week, or the hour.

The owners of these buildings were as interesting and varied as the tenants. They had, however, one thing in common: when overtures were made to purchase their properties, all assumed the prospective purchaser to be Simpsons, which was often, but not always, the case. When Simpsons *was* involved, negotiations were carried on by a trust company which went to great, but usually futile lengths to keep our identity concealed, for it was expected, of course, that Simpsons would pay a premium.

When four Metcalfe lots were acquired to provide Simpsons with breathing room on the west, interest in that street waned. Nonetheless some agent or other turned up every few months from 1966 to 1971, purporting to have exclusive rights to sell Ben's for the owners, the Kravitz brothers.

One of the Kravitz brothers' "agents," on my insistence, actually produced two of the brothers in my office to discuss the possibility of Simpsons purchasing Ben's. Nothing came of the meeting, because the numbers discussed initially turned out to be flexible – far more flexible on Ben's side than Simpsons'.

But, whereas Metcalfe could be taken or left, the Mansfield side was vital. Given the geography of Montreal and the location of competing stores – Eaton's, Morgan's (The Bay), Dupuis Frères, and Ogilvy's – it did not require too much imagination to realize that the area between Simpsons and Eaton's would be the focal point for future retail development in the city. An equally compelling factor was that Simpsons' link to Montreal's subway system would have to be at Boulevard de Maisonneuve. The possibility of a terminal that would stretch all the way from Simpsons, through Eaton's to The Bay, was an enticing concept.

By 1968, all the properties along Mansfield, except two, had been acquired. Each of the transactions bringing about this assembly required some strange negotiating, but the last two acquisitions were stranger than fiction. The unusual aspects of these transactions and the devices used to bring them to completion should interest real estate salesmen, purchasers, and sellers alike. Who knows? There may be lessons to be learned.

Simpsons' agent in most of the purchases of the properties north of the store was the Royal Trust Company. One of the Royal Trust's real estate men was a superior salesman who knew his products. He was much more than just a salesman, he was a psychologist. In addition to his knowledge of real estate, he learned everything he could about his clients, buyers, and sellers. The financial situation, the family situation, the habits of the owners, and, hopefully, the sellers of properties, were carefully studied. This knowledge he used with great skill to consummate what would otherwise be impossible deals. And he needed all his knowledge and know-how to acquire for Simpsons the two vital parcels of land on Mansfield Street.

The two properties required by Simpsons on Mansfield Street between the north side of the store and Boulevard de Maisonneuve, were one building in the middle of the block, and the restaurant-bar-hotel complex on the northeast corner, known as Monsieur Neptune – Father Neptune to the anglophones.

The property in the middle of the block was owned by Charlie and Harry Shafter, who ran a large plumbing business on Dorchester Street that had been started by their father. For many years, Simpsons had made futile attempts to purchase the Shafter Brothers' property. My predecessor, Bob Gibson, and the Royal Trust briefed me well on the numerous offers Simpsons had made in the early sixties and the equally numerous failures which had ensued. So by 1966, when I went to Montreal, I was fully aware of the kind of man I would be dealing with in the person of Charles Shafter. I have no knowledge of how Charlie Shafter operated his plumbing business, but if it resembled his real estate dealings, I would prefer to unplug my own drains.

Prior to my involvement, every deal had fallen through because Charlie Shafter broke his word. Time after time, a verbal agreement as to price and terms would be reached, only to have Charlie raise the price when the document was presented to him for signing. His favourite increment was $25,000. On one or two occasions we agreed to the higher figure, only to have still another $25,000 tacked on. Our distrust of Charlie deepened with each incident. When I first entered the picture about 1966, I was informed that Charlie's brother Harry might be having health problems, and discreet inquiries indicated that the brothers might prefer cash in the bank to real estate holdings. The time was ripe, apparently, but I was determined not to be sucked in like previous Simpsons negotiators.

Royal Trust was instructed to inform Shafter that I simply would not tolerate any price increase once the deal was agreed upon. If he pulled one of his old tricks, he could forget about selling to Simpsons – ever. This, of course, was pure bluster. I knew, and I am sure Shafter knew, that we must buy eventually; however, it was a stance that had to be taken. An offer was negotiated at a very high price, because Montreal property values were still being buoyed by the Expo building boom. But Charlie reneged. He wanted more. How much more? The standard $25,000 of course. I was outraged, and refused to deal with Charlie Shafter – ever again!

In 1969 Harry Shafter died. By this time, Montreal's pre-Expo boom had turned into a post-Expo bust; downtown real estate was not moving. Harry's estate could use cash. The time again seemed ripe. Although my previous stance with Charlie had been pure and simple bluff and dealing once again with the scoundrel was inevitable, I was sure there was some way to avoid a repetition of past performances. "Can we not get him to sign on the spot, once a price is agreed upon?" I asked the Royal Trust man.

"Perhaps, if you allow me a wide enough price range in which to work," he replied. Why not? "Let us say we set a bottom figure ridiculously low enough to incense him, but allow you to double, or even triple the price. Would that have a chance?" I asked.

It was agreed. The low figure was set at about $130,000 less than that which had been accepted, then rejected previously. The high figure was set at $25,000 more than we ever expected to pay.

A document was prepared with two items missing — the price and the date. The Royal Trust man thoughtfully arranged a meeting which would allow for at least two hours of uninterrupted negotiation, and was armed with a certified cheque for $10,000. Charlie scarcely needed to be reminded of the poor business conditions in Montreal at the time. But he was, and by the time the initial offer was made, it may not have appeared to be so ridiculously low after all. The figures remain confidential, but Charlie agreed to a price $35,000 above the starting figure – $95,000 below the offer he had previously rejected, and even further below the outside limit which had been set. The document was whipped out, dated, and the price entered. Charlie signed. And that was that.

Salem Alepin owned the other property, the Monsieur Neptune, so vital to Simpsons' long-range plan for Montreal. He had friends and acquaintances in many high places – one was rumoured to be Maurice Duplessis, Quebec's dictatorial Premier of the forties and fifties. Certainly he seemed to enjoy privileges not available to other nearby restauranteurs. Neptune had the only liquor licence granted to a comparable establishment for blocks around, and it openly flouted closing laws, free from harassment by police or other civic authorities. He was also a shrewd businessman, so it is not surprising that under these circumstances Alepin accumulated a modest fortune. Among other things, he had a fishing camp in the Laurentians, to which he was often transported by helicopter. When not at his camp, he resided in a suite in the hotel above the bar, which in turn, was above the main-floor restaurant. The bar was his office. Each morning he arrived at the bar at about nine o'clock to begin writing cheques, checking invoices and attending to other bookkeeping details.

The Royal Trust real estate man knew all these facts, because he had been studying Monsieur Alepin for years. He also knew that he had children who probably could not or would not carry on the business. But it was his knowledge of yet another detail of Alepin's daily routine which was to be the key factor in effecting the eventual purchase of his property.

Alepin's began sipping brandy when he signed his first cheque, about nine each morning. About noon each day, Alepin would toddle back upstairs, returning late in the afternoon for more of the same. Thus, he had to be caught for a few moments of negotiation sometime between nine and eleven each morning. Patient beyond belief, our agent visited M. Alepin, day after painful day, in bursts of two or three weeks at a time, striking while the iron was presumed to be hot.

Although consideration of the property began years earlier, written documentation begins in 1965. At that time, a price twice that eventually paid was being kicked around. In 1968 though, during the post-Expo recession, things heated up and our man resumed his 9 a.m. attendance at Father Neptune's bar. Occasionally, at the very point when progress seemed assured, Alepin would helicopter up to his fishing camp and disappear for weeks at a time.

Eventually, substantial agreement on the selling price was reached, but Alepin insisted we lease back to him for three to five years. This was quite acceptable to Simpsons, but some of his terms were not. Moreover, details of the terms were about as volatile as the brandy fumes which clouded the atmosphere during negotiating sessions.

If Herb Tees, Jack Watson, and André Bourassa, of the notarial firm of McLean Marler Tees Watson & Associates, did not exactly enjoy the work, they must surely have appreciated the income, for they prepared innumerable drafts of the offer to purchase and the agreement to lease, only to have them rejected or modified to such an extent as to be unrecognizable.

At long last, on March 23, 1971, Salem Alepin signed. But, rather than bringing an end to the frustrating dealings with Monsieur Alepin, the signing proved to be only the beginning. Once again, new lease agreements had to be prepared as Alepin changed paragraphs and clauses. Among his important concerns was that the premises would be not known as Monsieur Neptune after his lease expired. After this was agreed to, he wanted the entire building demolished after his lease expired. And so it went, with Simpsons accommodating every whim, until about the middle of May, when it became necessary to threaten legal action. Finally, on June 8, he threw the ultimate bombshell. He would not sign a deed of sale unless we agreed to pay an additional $200,000. He claimed that a nearby parcel of land had been sold at a price which made his property worth the additional amount.

During the period between the signing of the agreement to purchase and Alepin's latest ultimatum, while we were agreeing to change after change, we were faced with a constant nagging worry. The agreement to purchase was not registrable against the title to the land at the land titles office for the district of Montreal. Alepin could, therefore, sell to another purchaser who would be unaware of Alepin's prior commitment to us. Instead of owning the property, which we desperately wanted, we would merely have a long, bitter lawsuit on our hands.

Legal action, which was being considered, ran into a bit of a snag. The agreement had been signed and the purchase was to be made for Simpsons by the Royal Trust Company. Although it was obvious to Alepin from the beginning that Simpsons was to be the purchaser, it was felt that it would do no good to admit this, and might well encourage him to seek an even higher price. Besides, our relations were often strained because of our demolition of properties adjacent to his. Under the circumstances, Simpsons was reluctant to sue under its own name. The Royal Trust Company positively refused to become involved in a lawsuit. But Alepin had to be forced to close the deal.

Our legal counsel, Arthur Weldon of Duquet, MacKay, Weldon, Bronsetter, Willis & Johnson, came up with the idea that we should form a new land holding company, to which Royal Trust would transfer the agreement to purchase and the lease agreement, which they were holding on behalf of Simpsons. The new company would then sue Alepin. And there would be a bonus. The transfer of the agreements to the new company would be registrable, thus putting an encumbrance on the title, which would prevent or discourage the sale of the property to anyone else. Jokingly, I suggested to Arthur Weldon that the name of the new company should be The Monsieur Neptune Acquisition Company, Inc. But to keep Neptune in the picture, Neptal Properties Limited was the final choice.

Armed with our new weapons, a new approach was made to Alepin through his notary. It was made plain that he faced a long, expensive lawsuit if he failed to live up to his agreement. There may also have been a suggestion that he may well find his customers somewhat inconvenienced by the noise and dirt of demolition, which could conceivably take place next door. A few mornings later, sometime after 9 a.m., but before reaching his quota of Martell's most famous product, the deed of sale was formally executed.

Alepin carried on until his lease expired, made sure the building, along with the Father Neptune name, would be destroyed, and shortly thereafter, died. His death may well have been the result of a broken heart because he really loved that place. It was said that he sometimes believed he *was* Father Neptune and would not go the way of the mortals with whom he did business.

*   *   *

During one period of expansion, Simpsons Montreal store's efforts to provide a car parking facility had a most unexpected result. In 1953 and 1954, A. H. Lofft, general manager, was directing an expansion program which was to nearly double the store's selling area.

Our major competitors, a few blocks to the east, had much larger sales areas than Simpsons and were supported by adjacent parking lots. Simpsons had no parking facility of any kind and, while the expansion would close the gap somewhat in respect to selling space, acquiring an appropriate parking area was vital and was given first priority.

At that time, I was merchandise manager of the store. Although my responsibilities in the expansion programme were primarily concerned with merchandising new selling areas, I somehow became Lofft's man in search of parking. I inspected several nearby buildings which could be demolished so that the land might be used for surface parking. I also researched pigeonhole and other mechanical parking garages, and explored every other idea anyone suggested.

In those days I commuted daily from my home in Mount Royal on a Canadian National Railways train. The line ran through a tunnel under Mount Royal, terminating at Central Station, a long city block from our store.

A very short city block of perhaps three-hundred feet from the store, the tracks emerged from the tunnel into a huge excavation. It was fifty feet deep to track level and, except for a narrow building on Cathcart Street (the tunnel end), occupied a full city block bounded by Cathcart on the north, Dorchester Street on the south, Mansfield on the west, and St. Monique Street, a southerly extension of McGill College Avenue, on the east.

Every day as I walked from Central Station to the store in the morning and from the store to the station in the evening, I travelled along Mansfield, gazing down into the hole, as did most passers-by. On summer days these spectators gathered on the street, fascinated by lawn-mowing operations. The grass on the steeply sloped banks, from street level to track level, was cut by rolling reel mowers down the incline, on the ends of long ropes. By manipulating the ropes with great skill, an operator guided each mower as it roared downward, and then pulled it back to the top for another run. The watchers on the street sometimes bet that a swath would not have the proper overlap, leaving a strip of grass uncut. They seldom won!

One day, as I walked past the excavation, I was dazzled by the obvious: all we had to do to have the best department store parking garage in North America was to fill in the hole with layers of parking decks.

I rushed to Mr. Lofft's office with the news that our parking problem was solved. I also pointed out that, since he walked by the cavity twice each day on his way to and from lunch at the St. James's Club, we might have saved ourselves much time and effort if either of us had been more imaginative than to look into the excavation with unseeing eyes.

About that time, William Zeckendorf, the innovative New York real estate development tycoon, was very much in the business news. *Fortune, Newsweek,* and other periodicals had published articles that featured him and his firm, Webb & Knapp. Lofft and I had read and discussed these stories. Lofft was so impressed by Zeckendorf's accomplishments that, in reply to my recommendation that we arrange with the owners, Canadian National Railways, to use the "hole" as a parking facility, Lofft immediately suggested that this was a project for Mr. Zeckendorf. I could see no reason why we should not start with the CNR, but I concluded our initial discussion by agreeing that Zeckendorf was indeed accomplishing things in core areas of big cities.

The following morning, I asked Marie Rivet, then Mr. Lofft's secretary and some years later mine, for an appointment with Mr. Lofft. She said he was out of town and had no idea when he would return.

A few days later, however, Mr. Lofft called me into his office and announced, "Well, I saw the great man." Then with a gesture he often used when in a conspiratorial mood, he put his left hand to the right side of his mouth and whispered, "And, between you and me, he is one of the biggest bullshitters and frauds I have ever met."

At that moment, "great man" meant nothing to me; I had not twigged to whom he could be referring, and the derogatory appraisal which followed did not seem appropriate from Lofft. At that time, the great men in my life, and presumably his, were C. L. Burton, chairman of the board, and E. G. Burton, president of Simpsons! Lofft's great man, however, turned out to be Mr. Zeckendorf.

Following our discussion a few days earlier, Lofft had telephoned Zeckendorf and arranged to meet him in New York the next day. Mr. Zeckendorf was indeed interested in the "hole" – so interested, in fact, that it was agreed that Mr. Lofft would arrange a meeting of Zeckendorf, the late Donald Gordon, then president of Canadian National Railways, and the late E. G. Burton, then president of Simpsons.

After Lofft returned to Montreal, he wrote to Mr. Burton about the planned meeting. Miss Rivet vividly recalls Lofft writing, "If anyone thinks he has a hand with God at making the world, it is Zeckendorf."

For many years, I had intended to document this story for this book, as well as for Simpsons historical records. When Donald Gordon died in 1970, I realized that the only person who could verify Simpsons involvement was Mr. Zeckendorf. Mr. Lofft died in 1966, Mr. Burton in 1968, and Simpsons files had been destroyed after the latter's death. Accordingly, I began what I thought would be a small research project in the summer of 1970, by asking a friend in the CNR's executive offices to search their files, and by writing two letters to Mr. Zeckendorf. The small research project took five years.

After my friend at the CNR informed me that all the railroad's files on this subject had been destroyed when the head office had moved into a new building, I decided to communicate directly with Mr. Zeckendorf. On August 11, 1970, I wrote him as follows:

Some time ago, in 1952 or perhaps in 1953, when I was his assistant, the late Mr. A. H. Lofft who was then General Manager of the Robert Simpson Montreal Limited, visited you in your office in New York. As a result of this visit, I am sure you will remember, a meeting was arranged at which you, the late Mr. Donald Gordon, then president of the CNR, and the late Mr. E. G. Burton, then president of Simpsons Limited were present.

The reason for the meeting was that Simpsons was interested in locating a parking garage between Central Station and the Mount Royal Tunnel entrance. Mr. Lofft, of course, realized that it would be necessary to have a building of some proportions over the parking areas. It was for this reason that he approached you. While nothing came of the parking garage idea, I am sure that your meeting with Donald Gordon and Mr. Burton eventually resulted in the building of the Queen Elizabeth Hotel and Place Ville Marie.

Simpsons will be celebrating its 100th anniversary in 1972 and I am quite anxious to document these events. Could I impose on you to take a few minutes to drop me a line and let me have details that you can recall in regard to this meeting. Any information you may provide will be sincerely appreciated.

Incidentally, my friends at the CNR tell me that the files in respect to the meeting were destroyed when they moved into their new quarters from McGill Street. There is now merely a card which indicates that a file "Simpsons, CNR Parking Garage" has been destroyed.

With all good wishes.

Sincerely,
J. S. Bryant

Little did I know that four days later, on August 15, the *Montreal Star* would begin a series of articles excerpted from Mr. Zeckendorf's about-to-be published autobiography, containing his version of his association with Donald Gordon and the CNR. Thus, on August 17, 1970, I hastened to write a second letter to Mr. Zeckendorf:

> This is further to my letter of August 11, 1970.
>
> I was naturally impressed by the coincidence of the publication of the series of articles, reprinted from a book you have written, which began on Saturday, August 15, in the *Montreal Star.*
>
> I just want to assure you that I had no inkling whatsoever that the articles or the book were on the way.
>
> I note that my thoughts on the beginning of your association with the Canadian National Railways do not gibe with your book. However, many people, such as secretaries, remember details of Mr. Lofft's visit to you, and the susbsequent meeting between you and the late Donald Gordon and the late E. G. Burton, and I am sure these were important factors in your involvement with Place Ville Marie.
>
> I would very much appreciate hearing from you.
>
> Sincerely,
> J. S. Bryant

Since neither letter was ever acknowledged or returned, I was forced to look elsewhere for confirmation of my version. In the summer of 1975, while I was authenticating a number of incidents in this book, I studied Zeckendorf's autobiography. He does not mention meeting Donald Gordon as a result of Lofft's visit. Instead, he proclaims that the association began when Senator Thomas Viene of Montreal and a Montreal realtor, Rudolph Lemire, called on him. In his book, Zeckendorf allows Viene and Lemire to drop out of sight without mentioning a date, or further dealings with them. He does refer to Webb & Knapp considering Canada in 1955 and later refers to talks with Gordon in the summer of 1955.

But, I knew that Lofft had visited Zeckendorf when Simpsons search for parking was most intense – as early as the fall of 1953 and no later than April 1954 when I was appointed general manager of Simpsons in Halifax. Where, I wondered, would I find some evidence, however slight, that my memory had not been playing tricks on me all these years?

As a last resort I turned to the CNR's head-office library. It is under the direction of Helene Dechief, systems librarian. A former Simpson employee, Miss Dechief took an intense interest in my problem, but she was able to find in the library only one reference to Mr. Gordon's first meeting with Mr. Zeckendorf. That was in a speech Gordon made to Rensselaer Polytechnic's School of Architecture on April 10, 1964, in which he stated, "Mr. Zeckendorf was referred to us by an intermediary."

But Miss Dechief could not believe that memos and letters written personally by Donald Gordon on such an important subject could have been destroyed. And she was right! These files were found and made available to me.

I began to read with some apprehension. Would I find the clue for which I was searching?

The first letter written by Mr. Gordon to a CNR vice-president on the subject was dated October 22, 1953. It refers to a talk he had had with E. G. Burton about a parking garage which might be included in the CN's plans for "the development north of Dorchester." No mention of Mr. Zeckendorf.

A gap of two years followed. Was I to be disappointed again? On October 19, 1955, a memo to Mr. Gordon from a W.S. confirmed a luncheon engagement at the Mount Royal Club in Montreal for October 26, 1955. The purpose of the meeting was for Mr. Burton and Mr. Lofft "to speak to you [Mr. Gordon] once again on a matter which they discussed some two years ago." Again nothing about Zeckendorf. But wait! In a corner of the memo is a somewhat-faded pencilled note in Mr. Gordon's own hand. It reads: "They would like me to talk to Zeckendorf."

At last, Zeckendorf was connected to Simpsons! But what had happened between October 1953, about the time Lofft and Zeckendorf met, and October 1955? Although Mr. Gordon's pencilled note might suggest that he had not met Zeckendorf by October 19, 1955, this could not very well be true. A final memo from Mr. Gordon, addressed: "Note for file," dated December 7, 1955, includes, "Since my luncheon of October 26 with Mr. Burton the question of the Webb & Knapp appointment has not progressed very far."

Clearly, that note indicates that talks had been taking place over a long period of time, quite possibly since October 1953, the date of Gordon's first memo which must have resulted from Lofft's visit to

154

Zeckendorf. It is unlikely that an appointment would be considered in a matter of six weeks.

Did Zeckendorf attend the October 1953 meeting with Burton and Gordon? And, if so, was his presence so confidential that it was never documented?

The answer to these and many other questions only Zeckendorf could have provided. Now even he will not be able to do this. On October 1, 1976, just as this book was being put into production, William Zeckendorf died; but had he lived he could not dispute that he first learned of Montreal's development possibilities from Lofft and that Lofft was the intermediary. It was Mr. Lofft's visit to Mr. Zeckendorf, which I inadvertently catalyzed, that triggered the imaginative development over the "hole."

And imaginative it certainly was. Although the CNR had had plans for a railway terminal and hotel on the site from the time the property was acquired in 1912 by Sir William Mackenzie and Sir Donald Mann of the Canadian National Railways' predecessor, the Canadian Northern Railways, it was Zeckendorf who prepared the master plan which resulted in the construction of famed Place Ville Marie with its forty-five storey cruciform tower and vast pedestrian areas in the very heart of Montreal.

Place Ville Marie was responsible for two other developments which were to become important to Montreal. The first was the building boom which lasted from 1957 to Expo year 1967, enabling Montreal to maintain its position as Canada's number one metropolis. Moreover, Montreal's vast underground city was launched. The Place Ville Marie underground shopping promenade has grown to the point where pedestrians are now able to move from Place du Canada and the Château Champlain at Peel and Saint-Antoine Streets through Hotel Bonaventure, the CNR's central terminal, the Queen Elizabeth Hotel, and Place Ville Marie to University and Cathcart Streets. Altogether, there are ten miles of underground walkways and malls where Montreal pedestrians may shop, board trains, take the Metro, eat, be entertained, have a shampoo, a face lift, or a massage, free from summer heat and winter storms. And the concept has been contagious. Most new downtown buildings have their own subterranean developments, connecting with each other and with the Metro. There are now one hundred acres of underground city and Metro stations. Montreal may indeed look forward to the fulfilment of the dream of world-famed urban planner, Vincent Ponte, who helped Mr. Zeckendorf design Place Ville Marie. Mr. Ponte visualizes a city where *all* vehicular and foot traffic are separated, so that pedestrians walk in air-conditioned comfort or use underground subway systems while vehicles brave the weather. Thanks to Mr. Zeckendorf, Montreal is unique among the great cities of the world.

Zeckendorf provoked many critics, but none, I feel sure, accused him of minimizing his own accomplishments. Consequently, it is not surprising that he failed to reply to my letters. Perhaps he did not want anyone to detract from his chosen position as God's helper.

Although Simpsons' visions of a super parking garage were superceded by Mr. Zeckendorf's and Mr. Gordon's greater dreams, our store did eventually obtain a parking facility. It was a pigeon-hole-type, mechanical garage – about the only choice left to us in those days – and a disaster from the start.

The first problem was mechanical. The elevators which lifted automobiles to the stalls broke down continually, usually just before the store closed. If closing was at 5:30 p.m., the breakdown occurred at 5:00 p.m. On evenings when the store closed at 9:00, the stoppage was perversely delayed until 8:30.

In any event, Simpsons shoppers were left waiting for their cars, often on cold winter days, until repairs to the garage elevators could be effected. Sometimes it took hours to get things moving and, occasionally, customers were required to find other means of transportation to their homes and to return for their cars on the following day.

Needless to say this situation did not enchance the business of either Simpsons or the parking garage. Simpsons did not own the garage, but had backed a man named Emile Collette, a Montreal fabric wholesaler and entrepreneur, by guaranteeing the first half of a mortgage.

No sooner were the mechanical bugs brought under control than a new problem faced the ill-fated garage. When Simpsons was desperately searching for parking in the fifties, no suitable vacant lot could be found close enough to the store. Then, in 1962, Montreal began construction of its subway system. Building after building on Burnside (later renamed Boulevard de Maisonneuve), a street within one hundred feet of the garage, was expropriated and demolished. While waiting for construction to begin, and after it was completed, the resulting vacant lots were filled in and used for easy-access off-street parking. The competition was too great for the mechanical garage and one financial crisis followed another.

Finally, in 1967 another problem arose. Montreal's city fathers decided that Mansfield Street, on which the garage was located one block north of the store, should be turned into a one-way thorough-fare going north. This forced most prospective customers of the garage to take a long, circuitous route to the entrance. The majority of these drivers found more convenient parking nearer the stores of our competitors. About a year later, the traffic authorities were persuaded to compromise. Mansfield Street was again two-way for the short block on which the garage entrance was located, but by this time the damage had been done.

By 1969, it became obvious that the owners, Raymond Collette, who had taken over on the death of his brother, and his partner, a M. Pouliot, could make no further payments on the mortgage. Consequently, Simpsons would have been forced to take over, make the payments, and attempt to salvage whatever remained of the ill-advised investment.

But there was one other possibility. If Collette and Pouliot could find a purchaser prepared to pay a higher price than the mortgage amount, they could pocket the difference. I agreed to give them a month or two to look for such a buyer. One or two prospects emerged, but none with much financial stability. Moreover, the pro-bability of anyone paying more for the building than the amount of the outstanding mortgage became slimmer with each new prospec-tive buyer.

The likelihood of a new building boom beginning in downtown Montreal made it imperative that Simpsons keep the garage in oper-ation if possible. Under these circumstances, I undertook to do some searching for a suitable buyer. Since Simpsons had not, at the time, become legal owner and for other (mainly political) considerations, it seemed wise to keep knowledge of my activities from Messieurs Collette and Pouliot.

I began by researching the companies that were operating parking lots and garages in downtown Montreal. One had all the credentials required. Canadawide Parking not only was owned by Avis, but Avis (Canada) was partly owned by the United States corporate giant, International Telephone and Telegraph Company. Little chance that a deal with Canadawide would go financially sour!

I contacted my friend, Lawrie Adams, chairman of the board of Avis, and initiated some confidential negotiations. These discussions were supported by correspondence which came to me on Avis letterheads and was filed separately from the regular parking-garage records.

During this period, I met often with Collette and Pouliot to discuss progress and strategy, but I did not reveal the possible offer from Canadawide. In the course of one of the Collette-Pouliot meetings in my office, I asked my secretary for the parking-garage file so I could check on some detail of the mortgage. Mr. Collette was sitting on my right, Mr. Pouliot on my left – both within reading distance of the material on my desk. As I opened the folder, my heart sank. Had gremlins been at work? The first word I saw on the top document, printed in what seemed to be inches-high type, was AVIS.

Fortunately, my confusion and embarrassment went unnoticed by my companions. They were French, and the paper on top of the file was not from Avis, but a legal document written in French. For them, *avis* merely meant "notice."

In the end, the garage was sold to Canadawide (or Avis or IT & T, depending, I suppose, upon how one interprets the financial structures of these companies), at one of those wild meetings attended by about twenty-five people, including a dozen lawyers. The highlight of the conference was an interruption of some two hours, while an attorney tracked down Emile Collette's widow to obtain some sort of release. She was at a golf course! A fine golfer, she much preferred that activity to attending a meeting to sign away her interest in a white elephant.

Canadawide operated the garage until the spring of 1975. By that time, Simpsons parking needs were being satisfied by other facilities. When I visited Montreal in the summer of 1975, the building was being demolished. The land had become too valuable to be used for such a marginal enterprise. As Lawrie Adams remarked, "You could say that one parking garage was equal to three financial baths: one for Simpsons, one for Collette and Pouliot, and one for Avis."

The Terrorists

Canada first learned of the FLQ (The Quebec Liberation Front) on March 8, 1963, when the morning news reported that three Canadian Army military establishments in Montreal had been hit by Molotov cocktails. Before the bombs exploded, the letters FLQ had been painted on the walls of the buildings.

The FLQ's first public statement was distributed to the press the following day. It read:

NOTICE TO THE POPULATION
OF THE STATE OF QUEBEC

The Quebec Liberation Front (FLQ) is a revolutionary movement of volunteers ready to die for the political and economic independence of Quebec.

The suicide-commandos of the FLQ have as their principal mission the complete destruction, by systematic sabotage, of:

a) all colonial (federal) symbols and institutions, in particular the RCMP and the armed forces;

b) all the information media in the colonial language (English) which hold us in contempt;

c) all commercial establishments and enterprises which practise discrimination against Quebeckers, which do not use French as the first language, which advertise in the colonial language (English);

d) all plants and factories which discriminate against French-speaking workers.

The Quebec Liberation Front will proceed to the progressive elimination of all collaborators with the occupier.

The Quebec Liberation Front will also attack all American cultural and commercial interests, natural allies of English colonialism. All FLQ volunteers have on their persons during acts of sabotage identification papers for the Republic of Quebec. We ask that our wounded and our prisoners be treated as political prisoners in accordance with the Geneva Convention on the rules of war.

INDEPENDENCE OR DEATH

THE DIGNITY OF THE QUEBEC PEOPLE DEMANDS INDEPENDENCE.

QUEBEC'S INDEPENDENCE IS ONLY POSSIBLE THROUGH SOCIAL REVOLUTION.

SOCIAL REVOLUTION MEANS A FREE QUEBEC.

STUDENTS, WORKERS, PEASANTS, FORM YOUR CLANDESTINE GROUPS AGAINST ANGLO-AMERICAN COLONIALISM.

The Quebec Liberation Front which issued this communiqué was spawned in Quebec's universities and colleges, where young French Canadians blamed the English for all the Province's real and imagined woes. Attracted by the teachings of Marx, Mao, and others, they soon adopted revolutionary ideas and formed small cells, often unknown to each other, but all dedicated to separating Quebec from Canada. For seven years following the 1963 attacks they sporadically raided, robbed, bombed, and killed until the reign of terror reached a climax with the abduction of James Richard (Jasper) Cross, British Trade Commissioner in Montreal in the fall of 1970.

What were the thoughts and reactions of a person heading up one of Montreal's largest department-store organizations during the height of FLQ terrorism? What was it like to drive to work passing manned troop carriers at every other corner, knowing that a series of bomb threats may have to be faced upon arrival? To be sure, phone bomb threats were nothing new. They began years earlier, but the kidnapping had given them an even deeper significance. Although it should have been the year's busiest season, instore sales had slowed to a walk. Telephone order business, however was brisk because many customers were afraid to venture outside their homes. The telephones were also kept busy receiving bomb threats – some mornings as many as twenty – frequently only a few minutes apart. And none could be ignored, as one of our competitors sadly discovered. What was it like to be responsible for three stores, three warehouses, two hundred trucks, and the direction of as many as five thousand employees at peak seasons? I can tell you. It was pure and simple hell!

I am not a Trudeau admirer, but I believe his handling of the FLQ crisis, by proclaiming the War Measures Act, was absolutely superb. It was timely and forceful. The enemy could not miss the point. Later, of course, he came under criticism by all sorts of people and groups. Few of his critics, I suggest, were in the line of fire. I doubt if their companies were among those listed in the FLQ's infamous manifesto in which Simpsons, along with other department stores, were mentioned as targets to be attacked.*

To some extent, I was being conditioned for the climax of October 5, 1970, by events which occurred in the few years preceding the kidnapping of Jasper Cross, and the murder of Pierre Laporte, Quebec's Minister of Labour and Immigration.

I had been with Simpsons in Montreal on and off since 1946. My last stint in that city began in 1966, and within a year I was faced with what may have been the greatest armed robbery in department store history. On April 17, 1967, four men with sub-machine guns concealed themselves near the sub-basement cash room. They relieved two Brink's guards of canvas bags containing close to half a million dollars in cash and cheques, fired a shot into the ceiling to demonstrate they meant business, and escaped. They were never apprehended; but then, Montreal robbers rarely are.

At that time, most bank holdups in the city occurred on Fridays. News broadcasters jokingly referred to these thefts as withdrawals to provide cash for the bandits' weekend activities. Our holdup occurred early on a Monday morning, causing one wit to comment that our 'visitors' must have lost a bundle at the races and couldn't wait until their own bank opened to replenish their funds.

This event was soon followed by one somewhat more upsetting. My wife and I returned to our Outremont home about eleven o'clock one evening, after a visit to Expo, to find the neighbourhood in an uproar. Police cars were everywhere and policemen were running around shining searchlights into back yards, hedges and lanes. Our home was teeming with young guests – classmates of our son, Tony, and our daughter, Bev.

* "We are terrorized by the capitalist Roman church, even though this seems to be diminishing (Who owns the property on which the stock exchange stands?), by the payments to reimburse Household Finance; by the publicity of the grand masters of consumption like Eaton, Simpson, Morgan, Steinberg, and General Motors."

It took us some time to understand what was going on, because everyone talked at the same time. Pieced together, the story went something like this: four men had broken into a home across the street, the owner being away at the time. What the intruders did not know was that the home had a burglar alarm system hooked up to the local police station. Even with this advantage, the police failed to capture the thieves in the case. As they entered the front door, the men burst past them and ran into our rather large yard. Shots were fired on both sides; other police cars were called and the search was on.

The young people in our house were oblivious to what had been taking place. But when the police knocked on our door to make sure that none of the fugitives had entered the house, some of the youngsters foolishly* went outside to join the search. Our daughter Bev noticed a man lying in the hedge and pointed him out to the police. An exchange of shots sent her scurrying back into the house, followed by the woman next door (who scared the life out of the girl by telling her to keep her face hidden, because the burglars would come after her when they were released from prison).

The man in the hedge was shot in the leg before being taken into custody. Another was picked up nearby, but two who had escaped were the object of the search going on when we arrived on the scene. These were arrested later, and all were sentenced to prison.

Although the FLQ had robbed an Outremont home in June, 1966, and had conducted many robberies to finance their activities, this event was not linked in any way to them. But it was not easily forgotten, because it brought terrorism right into our home. We became personally involved in Montreal's rush toward anarchy.

Meanwhile, the FLQ continued the bombings, which had begun on March 7, 1963, with the Molotov cocktail attacks on three military bases. Between that date and the opening of Montreal's Expo, four years later, the FLQ carried out a series of bombings which outraged the nation. A watchman and a secretary were killed by these bombs, an army sergeant (a demolition expert) maimed for life, and a terrorist accidentally blew himself up. The National Revenue building, the Canadian National station, the CNR's main line, and the television tower on Mount Royal were all FLQ targets.

For years, Montreal's retail sales had responded to both political

* Son Tony, now a lawyer, objects to this description.

and business conditions, going up or down, roller-coaster fashion, with good news or bad news. On rare occasions, when news was good on both the political and economic fronts, a minor boom resulted. Nineteen sixty-seven was such a year.

Except for President de Gaulle's outburst, "Vive Montréal, Vive le Québec, Vive le Québec Libre," which momentarily elated the separatists, things were quiet on the political front. Besides, many FLQ leaders were in jail. Expo visitors kept stores' cash registers humming. But, the higher the peak, the deeper the valley, and 1968 was to become a vintage year for FLQ bombings and general terrorism through telephone threats. The year started rather slowly, but heated up as harvest time approached. On June 24, 1968, the St. Jean Baptiste parade deteriorated into a riot, as police and separatists battled each other. Prime Minister Trudeau, who had denounced the separatists vigorously, was in the reviewing stand. He became the target of separatists' shouts and missiles. When police intervened, the paraders surged down side streets from Sherbrooke Street, the parade route, to the central business district.

The following morning, Montreal looked back to a night of terror in which scores were injured by stones, bottles, acid, and iron bars. Police cars were burned. Simpsons was spared on that occasion, but many stores had display windows broken.

That fall of 1968 proved to be the most difficult period endured by department stores, during the seven years (1963-1970) of terrorism. Montreal was in a post-Expo business slump. A mood of depression pervaded the retail community, which Simpsons could not escape. Eternal optimism is a quality which every good merchant is supposed to possess, and in the fall of 1968, as in every fall, hopes were buoyed up by the approach of cold weather and Christmas sales. But those hopes were not to be fulfilled.

Department stores think of particular dates much as a small child thinks of a birthday, and stores are often childishly literal minded. If an exceptional sales figure is achieved on a particular day of a particular year, sales must not merely be equalled, but bettered in the following year. Moreover, stores are slaves to the day of the week. If the Great May Sale began on a Tuesday last year, it must begin on Tuesday this year. But since an uncooperative calendar changes Tuesday, May 1 in one year, to Tuesday, April 30 in the following year and April 29 in the year after that, the Great May Sale sometimes takes place in April. This should explain a phenomenon which has puzzled department store customers for years.

But sometimes fate intervenes to select a date on which sales are to be lower in each succeeding year. The fateful date for Montreal stores was to be October 7. On that Monday in 1968, just as retailers expected the fall buying surge to begin, three hundred sticks of dynamite were stolen from a construction company's suburban site. The theft touched off a wave of bomb threats and actual bombings, which kept Montrealers on edge for the next two years.

Between October 7 and the end of the year, store executives were kept in a continuous state of anxiety. Phoned bomb threats rained on Simpsons and other department stores every day. On some days, dozens of calls were received, stating that bombs had been placed in the store; often a time for the promised explosion would be mentioned. And we knew that these were not idle threats. The Union Nationale Club Renaissance, the Liberal Club de Réforme, Domtar, Standard Structural Steel, the home of Charles Hershorn, president of Murry Hill, the transportation company, were all targets of the bombers. Some exploded; some were defused.

To appreciate fully the terror created by these bomb threats, the operation of Simpsons' telephone system should be explained. Two telephone numbers are used: one for administrative purposes and the other for taking orders telephoned in by customers. Calls to the first number come into a general switchboard where eight operators put the calls through to the office requested by the caller. Calls to the second number are handled by a sophisticated automatic system which takes each call in turn from a customer wishing to order or return merchandise, and stacks up the calls in sequence when all the order-takers are engaged. The administrative number is rarely used by the general public as it is available only in the telephone directory. The second number is shown in every Simpsons' newspaper advertisement and is widely known by most Montrealers. Thus, close to 100% of the bomb threat calls were taken by the women on the order desks.

On the average business day, 180 such desks are in operation. Most of the order-takers are married women who work part time; because of days off, evening openings, and hours of work designed to allow them to take care of home and family responsibilities, a roster of 375 is required. All the desks face the same way in a huge room

100' long by 50' wide. A wall-size blackboard on which daily instructions are printed in letters large enough to be read with ease 100' away, creates a community spirit in much the same way as the village bulletin board does.

In adjacent rooms, another forty people process orders phoned in by customers, and operate the main switchboard. Altogether, more than four hundred women have been brought together in one small corner of the St. Catherine Street store. A small community of women who have much in common has been created. They are all fluently bilingual, French being the mother tongue of most. Nearly all have families, and started their part-time career after the youngest child was sent off to school. Most have been at the job for several years, many have over twenty years of service.

But there is another force that brings them together. It is in the person of Mrs. Katherine French, manager of telephone services. Mrs. French, one of the brightest members of Simpsons' management team, is an organizational genius with contagious enthusiasm. Hovering over her large staff like a den mother, she has created a highly disciplined organization in an informal family-like atmosphere.

So it was in October 1968, when terrorists first began to attack Montreal department stores. Years later, order-takers like Mrs. Gilberte Gauthier and Mrs. Irene Bouchard, vividly remember the terrifying fear they encountered when the first calls were received. One fainted, another trembled for some minutes while Mrs. French and her assistant, Mrs. Mary Webster, tried to calm her. One, Mrs. Anne Bourdon, remembers receiving a threat the day after Eaton's was bombed. She was ill for a month with what doctors eventually diagnosed as an allergy attack brought on by the fright. Of course, a good many of the order-takers were fortunate enough to be spared receiving an actual phone call, but in that closely knit group they were not spared the fear which pervaded the entire telephone organization. The terror did not end with the day's work but spread to the homes, where children and husbands often pleaded with the mother not to go to work at Simpsons.

One incident is reminiscent of wartime heroics during the bombing of London in World War II.

Shortly before 1 p.m. Mrs. Muriel Comte, a switchboard operator, received one of the infrequent calls to come to the board rather than to the desk of an order-taker. The caller informed her that bombs would explode at precisely 2 p.m. Without hesitation, Mrs. Paula Dubi, switchboard supervisor, rearranged lunch hours so that a full staff would be on hand at 2 p.m. to take care of any emergency in case the telephoned threat turned out to be the real thing. Mrs. Comte remembers being one of those sent scurrying off to lunch with an admonition to be back before two o'clock. She also remembers being unable to eat.

Although not completely unexpected, some confusion followed the first call. It was taken by an order-taker and relayed to the office of the store superintendent by Mrs. French. The store's security people began a search of stair wells, elevator lobbies, escalator landings, exposed displays, and other locations to which the terrorists would have easy access. But, while this search was taking place, another call was received, then another. Obviously the security staff could not check out eleven floors of a huge building every few minutes.

A meeting of all senior executives was called – a sort of council of war – to plan a defence that would be effective without alarming our customers and staff. Teams, made up of department managers and junior executives, were assigned to every floor. The public address system using a code made up of numbers and colours, was used to alert the floor teams to begin a search. After a few days' practice, the entire building could be covered in a few minutes. But, some new development took place every day, that would cause us to modify or refine the system. Accordingly, daily meetings of the "council of war" replaced the usual sales promotion meetings. Methods of working with the telephone company and police forces to identify the callers and the location of their telephones were discussed. Special fire-proof blankets to be used to throw over the parcels suspected of containing bombs, were designed and ordered. Eventually a detailed routine was developed (and printed) to make efficient, thorough, rapid searches and to evacuate the store and control crowds if such proved necessary by the finding of a bomb.

The police, at this point, were not of much help. They were inexperienced also and their immediate solution to any bomb threat was to evacuate the entire building. This was not only impossible but unwise. Impossible because employees and customers would not have returned to the building before another emptying of the store would have had to take place. Unwise because panic would certainly occur at some locations as customers on eight floors and employees on these floors, plus the three service floors, milled around escalators, elevators, and stairwells. Panic in such circumstances could be more deadly than an explosion. Stores soon learned to inform the police of the threats and make searches for bombs with their own organizations – organizations, soon made by practice more efficient than search squads provided by police, which would require some minutes to arrive on the scene and then would not know where to look without the help of store personnel.

One limited evacuation did take place at Eaton's. On a brisk November morning in 1968, a shoe box was noticed in the jewelry and watch department. The sales manager of the department took the lid off and saw with horror that it did indeed contain dynamite, wire, and a clock mechanism.

The sales manager then acted in a manner that was later described as both brave and foolish (brave if you were one of those present, foolish if you simply read about it in the papers). He picked up the box and placed it in a nearby stairway landing at the corner of University and St. Catherine Streets. He then got customers and employees out of the area, locked the adjacent entrance, and called the police. The police evacuated the basement, main and second floors while Sergeant Côté of the demolition squad defused the bomb less than ten minutes before it was timed to explode.

In March of the following year, as a result of a description provided by an employee of the Queen's Printer bookshop, which had been bombed ten days earlier, Montreal police arrested Pierre Paul Geoffroy in the act of making a bomb in his apartment. A violent revolutionary, Geoffroy admitted placing bombs in more than one hundred locations, including Eaton's jewelry department and the Montreal Stock Exchange. It was felt, however, that this particular bomb was not meant for Eaton's but that Geoffroy was on his way to another site when he decided to get rid of his package in a hurry.

The jewelry department sales manager's act of bravery was particularly significant because a few days earlier a bomb *had* exploded in Eaton's. It had been placed in one of the coin-operated lockers used by customers to hold luggage and other cumbersome items while shopping. The lockers were located beneath a wide escalator leading from the main floor to the basement and the explosion ripped the escalator from its moorings and did considerable damage to nearby fixtures. Although no one was injured, as the explosion took place at night, Eaton's bombs were pretty close to home. The tension at Simpsons continued to mount, partly because searches of our store occasionally did turn up suspicious-looking items which spread the fear that pervaded the telephone order organization into other areas of the store. Shortly after the bomb was found at Eaton's, a similar shoe box was found by a porter in Simpsons' jewelry department. Thinking it had been inadvertently left by a customer he took it to the main floor information desk; from there it was routinely sent to the lost and found department on the seventh floor. When the lost and found people saw it, and learned the location where it had been left, they scattered in all directions; the area was blocked off and the Montreal police demolition squad was called in. An explosion blanket was thrown over the box which was then taken from the store and placed in an armoured truck. It turned out that the box was being used for its intended purpose – it contained shoes, albeit an old pair, probably left by someone with a twisted sense of humour.

As the end of the year approached, Montreal retailers hoped they would never have another like it. Sol Nayman, who was assistant general sales manager of Simpsons Montreal at the time and is now manager of Simpsons' huge flagship store at Queen and Yonge in downtown Toronto, was prompted to make a prophetic statement. At a Christmas party he suggested that the way things were going there might not even be a Santa Claus next year.

Sure enough, as 1968 ended, terrorism resumed with the New Year's Eve bombing at City Hall. Explosions in the Bank of Nova Scotia building and in the visitor's gallery of the Montreal Stock Exchange injured some, but miraculously killed no one. Bomb threats continued at Simpsons, but by now were being handled routinely. Sales planning was again on the agenda for executive meetings. In 1969 bombings and bomb threats were frequently accompanied by street demonstrations. Some of Simpsons display windows were broken on March 28 by students attempting to make McGill a French institution, and on June 24, St. Jean Baptiste paraders again developed into mobs roaming the streets, destroying anything and everything in their path. Simpsons had a dozen windows broken on Metcalfe and St. Catherine Streets. But, the worst was yet to come.

Through the traumatic days of 1968 and the first half of 1969,

Simpsons Montreal management team, in the tradition of true merchants, retained a collective sense of humour. The wit of the group was Doug Avery, general merchandise manager, who always relieved the tension with a classic one-liner.

Before I left for an October vacation, Doug and I were joking about what "they" would do for an encore on October 7, 1969, to match the bombings which began as a result of the dynamite theft on that date in 1968. Our joke was based on the belief that no one, not even the FLQ could think up a reverse sales plan which would match the disastrous effect of the previous year's activities. The joke was on us.

On October 7, 1969, my wife and I returned to our apartment in Deerfield Beach, Florida, just in time for the late evening news. As the TV came into focus, an unforgettable picture greeted us. I had the feeling I was having a nightmare. On the screen were scenes the news cameras had taken of a raging mob breaking windows and looting Simpsons downtown Montreal store – *My* store. For some minutes, the news was devoted to similar activities throughout the downtown commercial district. But it was not, after all, the FLQ that had thought up a new and better way to ruin retail sales. This night of violence and terror, which made all the other street riots in the city resemble an eight year old's cake-throwing birthday party, had an unexpected source. To a man, the Montreal police force had gone on an illegal strike – and the firemen joined them.

Taxi drivers, who were at the time having a running battle with authorities and the Murray Hill Company over that company's exclusive right to serve Montreal's international airport, seized the opportunity to begin a mass demonstration at City Hall. Militant students joined them and a parade of taxis proceeded to the Murray Hill garage. Cars and buses were damaged and burned; the garage was fire bombed. A Quebec provincial policeman, one of a few who had been sent to the city by the provincial government in a futile attempt to provide police protection, was killed. The demonstrators then moved up to St. Catherine Street, where they were joined by bystanders in a long night of terror, looting, and violence.

Hundreds of windows were broken in retail stores, and the cost of looting and damage ran into hundreds of thousands of dollars. Montreal's police had brought the city one step closer to anarchy. Simpsons was a big loser.

Threatened legislation forced the police back to work, but the riots initiated another period of political and business unrest in the city. A pervasive atmosphere of gloom settled over the city, and consumers reacted as they always do when political situations shatter their confidence in the future – they stayed home in droves. So, in the fall of 1969, we were to have more of the same, and it was close to Christmas before normal retail activity resumed.

Shortly after the police returned to work they raided the offices of a number of organizations suspected of subversive activities. Literature and documents seized in these raids convinced civic authorities that a number of separatist organizations might well join together in armed revolution, involving assassinations and kidnappings.

Accordingly, the city considered placing a ban on public demonstrations. Before the ban took effect, however, on November 7 (precisely one month after the police strike riot), yet another street demonstration was to end up in an attack on the premises of insurance companies, banks, and other institutions in Montreal's financial district. A number of separatist organizations, militant unionists, and students began the march, demanding the freedom of two convicted FLQ leaders, Pierre Vallières and Charles Gagnon.

After the legislation outlawing demonstrations was passed, things settled down somewhat. Only a few sporadic bombings interrupted the Christmas season, but retailing received a permanent and traumatic setback. Eaton's Santa Claus parade, which had for years delighted children and fellow retailers alike, was cancelled never to return, as Sol Nayman had prophesied a year earlier.

The year 1970 began rather quietly. Gagnon and Vallières, released on bail, made inflamatory statements, likening the struggle of the FLQ in Quebec to the revolutionary movements of Vietnam, Palestine, and the US Black Power movement. While these statements in themselves seemed insignificant, it soon became clear that kidnapping and other forms of violence were on the minds of FLQ members. If more attention had been given to FLQ plans that police stumbled on earlier in the year, the kidnappings which were to take place in October may not have been so surprising. In February, police arrested two men in a truck which contained weapons, a wicker basket, and plans for the abduction of the Israeli Consul in Montreal. One of the men arrested was Jacques Lanctôt. He skipped bail and later participated in the kidnapping of Jasper Cross. In June, a police raid on an FLQ Laurentian hideout unearthed, along with arms and dynamite, a plan to kidnap the US Consul in Montreal.

Once again, the first Monday in October proved fateful for Montreal retailers. At 8:30 on the morning of October 5, 1970 the FLQ abducted Jasper Cross, from his home on the slopes of Mount Royal, setting off a new reign of terror that eventually resulted in the proclamation of the War Measures Act.

But the seizing of Jasper Cross was much more than a business setback and a nightmarish news story to our family. We had been friends of Jasper and his wife Barbara since 1955, when we were both stationed in Halifax. Their large house on Redpath Crescent had been the home of one of my predecessors in Montreal, Hartley Lofft. We had been guests of both families many times. A few days before the kidnapping we had spent a pleasant evening with the Cross's at the St. Helen's Island theatre, La Poudrière. Somehow all the concerns about the political and economic effects of the kidnapping were replaced by personal outrage.

The new wave of bomb threats set off by the abduction could not be ignored, however. Once again Simpsons tried to cope with hundreds of phone calls. It was believed at the time that most of the calls were hoaxes, but we had to deal with them as if they were the real thing.

The FLQ immediately issued a number of communiques demanding, among other things, release of political prisoners, transportation of abductors to Cuba, and $500,000 in gold bars. On October 7, another communique and a letter from Mr. Cross arrived at radio station CKLM again demanding that the entire text of their manifesto, which named Simpsons along with other companies and individuals as being responsible for Quebec's woes, be broadcast over all radio and TV stations, and printed in all newspapers. And it indicated that those named would be among the first targets of the revolution. With this demand, the manifesto was published.

On October 10, Pierre Laporte was kidnapped by what turned out to be an FLQ cell, operating independently of the Cross group. On October 16, the War Measures Act was proclaimed. Early the following morning 242 people suspected of terrorist activities were arrested.

On October 17, Pierre Laporte was murdered. The murder did something to shock both FLQ members and the hoaxers. The phoned bomb threats abruptly stopped!

On Sunday, October 18, Prime Minister Trudeau broadcast a second message to Canadians in which he said that the FLQ's attempt to shake the will of the people would be a complete failure. On October 19, police found the house in which Pierre Laporte had been held and identified some of his kidnappers. But it was not until November 6 that one of these men, Bernard Lortie, was arrested, but he identified his collaborators, Paul and Jacques Rose, and Francis Simard. All were convicted of the crime.

Finally, on December 4, Jasper Cross was rescued, in a deal which permitted his abductors refuge in Cuba.

Cross's release brought to an end yet another period of violence and terror in Montreal, and the week of October 7 was to be remembered in retail circles as the beginning of yet another decline in sales that lasted almost until Christmas. Again, department store executives wondered what "they" would do for an encore next year.

After 1970, labour unrest replaced terrorism in adversely affecting retail sales. But in 1976, in the Quebec provincial election of November 15, René Lévesque accomplished by the democratic process what the FLQ and other separatist organizations had been unable to do in thirteen years of violence. His Parti Québecois, dedicated to separating Quebec from Canada, won 70 of 110 seats in the National Assembly. After the election, retail sales in Montreal and, in fact, throughout Canada suffered a temporary decline while Canadians contemplated an uncertain future.

The Merchants

In every city a few men – business, political, and social leaders – make the decisions responsible for the economic well-being of the community. In successful department stores the decision-makers may function as financiers, administrators, lawyers, or accountants, but they must ultimately be merchants.

The personal attributes required to become a successful merchant are much the same qualities to be found in those who succeed in any professional, political, religious, or other business endeavour. A mixture of intelligence, honesty, integrity, optimism, enthusiasm, imagination, power of observation, ability to work hard, and dedication to the business, is considered vital when the subject is being discussed by highly placed personnel officials in the retail field. And the ability to convey ideas to subordinates must be included in the list. There is no greater menace in department store merchandising, in my opinion, than the merchandise manager who berates a young buyer about markup being too low or markdowns being too high without providing some guidance as to how these problems might be corrected.

Certainly great merchants of the past had their own pet ways to identify merchants. C. L. Burton felt the chosen must be imbued with "a sense of urgency," and so gave that title to his autobiography. His son, E. G. Burton, thought of merchants as the kind of storekeepers who put a display of umbrellas at the store entrance when it began to rain. Others believed a true merchant would pick up merchandise which had fallen on the floor, even in a competitor's store. For Timothy Eaton, it helped to be a teetotaller and Irish.

One quality a good merchant need not have is patience. If a store executive remains passive while the merchant across the street is selling a hot item by the thousands, while his store is out of stock, he is

173

doomed to failure. Many of the most successful merchants are known to be impulsive. Few, in my experience, have been top-notch bridge players.

But, while patience may inhibit merchandising, it is helpful in training personnel. To provide enough executives for the hundreds of new stores being opened, department stores, as noted earlier, have abandoned the apprenticeship system, and resorted to intensive on-the-job training methods as the only viable alternative. Some members of my generation find this painful. It is difficult for them to believe that a good manager could be only two years out of college, with his assistant appointed yesterday. It is as if the blind are leading the blind – which reminds me of a shaggy-dog story about two salesmen: they were travelling a dusty road on the western prairies when it started to rain. They had learned that if their car were allowed to stop in any sort of depression in the road, the chances of moving it forward again in the gumbo mud were slim indeed. Their desperate need was to reach the nearest town, Pedunck, with its gravel roads, but they did not know the shortest route.

The salesmen hailed a farmer working in an adjacent field. Slowing the car, but not allowing it to stop, they called out, "Where is the road to Pedunck?"

"I don't know," the farmer shouted.

When they reached the end of the field, they decided to turn right on a sectional road which bisected theirs. At this point, the farmer came running across the angle of the field with another man in tow. He waved at them vigorously. The salesmen slowed up to allow the men to catch up with them. As the car sank slowly into a mud hole, with insufficient momentum to roll out, the salesmen heard the farmer call out:

"This is my brother. He doesn't know either."

With or without patience good merchandisers do not, of course, require all the personal qualities mentioned here, but some combination of them is vital. And those who are blessed with that priceless but undefinable asset, common sense, have a better than average chance to be successful.

One other characteristic has been possessed by almost all the superior merchants it has been my good fortune to know, or be associated with – a sense of humour. More particularly, these men and women have had the ability to laugh at themselves, and to couple their ability to see the funny side with that of eternal optimism. The true merchant forever believes that as things cannot get worse, they must get better.

Regardless of personal qualities possessed by individual department store executives, their decisions, if the enterprise is to be successful, must be based on merchandising considerations. In the end selling goods acquired from manufacturers, and selling services through store facilities, are the only assets a store has. Even profits made in credit operations depend on sales of merchandise or services. So, no matter in what area of the business a department store executive may function – financial, research and planning, credit, personnel, building maintenance – and no matter what his title, he is as much dependent on merchandising as the fellow who buys, sells or promotes the sale of sheets and pillow cases. Everyone employed by a department store is, or should be, a merchant. He or she will probably be a better merchant if endowed with a sense of humour and an optimistic outlook. With this in mind, a section on merchants and humour seemed an appropriate way to wind up this book.

One of the first great merchants I experienced was Robert Simpson. Robert Simpson of the Hudson's Bay Company, that is, not *the* Robert Simpson, who was somewhat, though not much, before my time. Simpson's sense of humour was somewhat subdued, but his optimism and enthusiasm were not. He promoted huge purchases of merchandise during the depression years, when almost everyone else was convinced that no one would buy anything. When he made one of his big buys, he would rush to the general manager, demanding full pages of newspaper space, all the display windows, banners on the selling floor, and any other promotional gimmick that he or the advertising department could think up. And, just as the first Robert Simpson had done in the earliest days of the Canadian department store, he wrote his own advertising copy.

Like many good merchants, Simpson was a sucker for salesmen and often allowed their contagious enthusiasms to infect him. Once, during the early depression years, when he was manager of the china and glassware department of the Hudson Bay's Calgary store, he had a visit from a representative of a glassware manufacturer. The salesman demonstrated the wonder of the glass industry – an unbreakable tumbler. He threw the sample drinking glass on the floor a dozen times, and while somewhat more noisy than a rubber ball, it bounced around quite as harmlessly. Simpson promptly purchased a carload. When the shipment arrived, he rushed to the office of the store's general manager, a man named Johnston, and demanded a full page of advertising in both daily newspapers, all the display windows along Eighth Avenue and along First Street West, and lots more. "Look," Simpson cried, "it's a miracle. It is just not possible to break these tumblers. We'll sell the whole carload in one day." With that, he threw a sample he had in his hand onto a margin of hardwood floor not covered by the deep-pile oriental rug. The glass shattered into thousands of pieces. Simpson stared at the wreckage in horror. The promotion went ahead, with a slight revision in the advertising copy – the word "virtually" being inserted in front of the word "unbreakable."

A few weeks later, with the tumblers disposed of and the incident forgotten, another salesman arrived. This one was selling dinnerware made by what was purported to be a revolutionary new technique. The plates simply could not be broken in ordinary use. To demonstrate, the salesman rolled plate after plate down a long aisle of the department, as if he were throwing bowling balls. The plates would crash against the wall at the end of the aisle with a resounding noise, but they would not break. Once again Simpson rushed for his order book. But, before he had time to visit Johnston's office with news of his latest huge purchase and promotional plans, Johnston appeared on the selling floor. Simpson rolled a plate down the aisle as the salesman had done. As the plate disintegrated, Johnston, a tall man, looked down at Simpson and disdainfully shouted, "For God's sake, Simpson, have you nothing better to do than to go around breaking your nice merchandise?"

But Simpson did have better things to do. He was promoted to the Winnipeg store where he later told me this story in order to ease the tension brought on by some merchandising setback and embarrassment I had suffered.

Looking back, I believe that Simpson's ability to laugh at himself, and to use the story to train his subordinates, must have had a last—ing effect on me. For as years went on, I found that injecting humour into training programmes was indeed an effective means of getting across a principle. I developed a library of merchandising humour, some of which was autobiographical, and some from sources so long forgotten that I came to believe that the stories were the products of my own imagination. Here is a part of my collection:

Principle: If the price is not right, the customers won't buy.

Story: A bartender in a New York bar was surprised one day to find a kangaroo sitting on one of the stools. The kangaroo asked for a scotch and soda. When served, the kangaroo said, "How much?" "Two dollars," replied the bartender. "Two dollars!" said the kangaroo in amazement. "That's a very high price." "Well, it's our price; this is a very high-class place," was the bartender's response. The kangaroo reached into his pouch and slammed two dollars on the counter. As he was putting the money in the cash register, the bartender looked in the mirror behind the bar to make sure he was not having an hallucination, but there the kangaroo was, sipping his drink. To make conversation, the bartender remarked, "You know, we don't see many kangaroos around here." "No bloody wonder at two dollars for a scotch and soda," replied the kangaroo indignantly. (Years later, the kangaroo turned up in a bar in his native Australia – or so said a newspaper clipping sent to me by an old friend and Simpson associate in Halifax, Ray Gaetz. He was apparently as price conscious as ever. According to the story, he ordered beer.)

Principle: If the mark-up is not high enough the store goes broke.

Story: On a rainy weekend, a cottager in the Laurentians went to the local village to buy some clay pipes, which could be used to keep the children quiet blowing bubbles. The storekeeper placed a wooden box containing the pipes, packed in sawdust, on the counter and asked the man to help himself, while he attended to another customer. The cottager selected a half dozen pipes, and asked the price. "Nickel each," came the reply from the other end of the store. "That seems pretty cheap," the customer remarked. "Would you mind telling me how much you pay for them? I was in this sort of business years ago." "You're an old customer," the storekeeper said, "so I'll tell you – 60¢ a dozen." "You pay 60¢ a dozen and sell for 5¢ each. You can't make much money doing that." "Ah," replied the storekeeper, "but we always break a few."

Principle: You can't sell what you don't have.

Story: When a buyer declares that *his* department has no demand for an item that is being sold by every other store in town, ask him if he ever heard of the dog that didn't eat meat. There was one once – because the family that owned him wouldn't buy him any!

Principle: New fixtures and decor won't sell merchandise unless the merchandise is what customers want or need. (Department store managements seem to have difficulty projecting accurately profit potential in relation to capital expended refurbishing store departments. This has been so in the past. It is so today. All too often it is not new carpeting and fixtures that are required, but new merchandise and merchandising. Unwise capital spending to create something new frequently causes an increased rent load, which is sure to keep the department in a loss position for years.)
Story: When unnecessary refurbishing of a department is proposed, ask how many store fixtures have been sold lately.

Principle: Merchandise that is not selling eats up profits. It must be marked down immediately, disposed of, and replaced by goods that will sell.
Story: A farmer told a friend that he had bought some pigs in June for twenty-five dollars each and sold them in August. "How much did you get for them in August?" his friend inquired. "Twenty-five dollars each" was the reply. "You can't make much money that way," said the friend. "Perhaps not," the farmer replied, "but I had the use of the pigs all summer."

Principle: Stores that buy more than they sell, go bankrupt.
Story: Assume that the selling department is a deep bathtub and the buyer is the bather. The down-drain represents sales, and the faucet represents purchases. If the faucet (purchases) is allowed to run at a faster rate than the down-drain (sales) takes the water away, the tub fills up and the bather (buyer) drowns.

Relieving tensions by injecting some humour into difficult business situations is about the best method of keeping department store disease at bay, and it is practiced throughout the merchandising game. After World War II, I made a number of trips to Europe with a fellow-buyer from Toronto, Norman Agar. Our first trip was orientation under the direction of one of Simpsons' most experienced buyers, Mary Lawson. About to retire, she was making her thirty-fourth Atlantic crossing on behalf of the company, her yearly visits to European markets being interrupted only by the war. Among other things, we purchased huge quantities of lace by the yard. Lace at that time was a best-selling item, highly profitable, but about as tedious an item to buy as any in the inventory of a large store. Samples were in huge albums, about twice the size of the largest family bible. Each pattern was shown with all the styles, edgings, insertions, beadings, galloons, in all the widths from ¼ inch to 3 inches, glued to a set of facing pages.

After flipping over forty or fifty pages, every pattern began to look alike, except to Mary Lawson, to whom the slightest variation in the arrangement of threads was as distinctive as the eyebrows of identical twins to their mother.

Norman was Mary's assistant and heir apparent and, as such, was required to write up orders as Mary barked instructions at a rate that would floor the average court stenographer. I represented Montreal, and my buyer there, Grace Packenham, with almost as much experience as Mary Lawson, had prepared for me a small notebook, containing samples of patterns and quantities required. All I had to do was to stand to one side as the pages were flipped over, and spot the patterns that matched closely. I could then make up my orders at my leisure. But Norman knew that he must have all the orders from a day of inspecting samples – translated from dozens of yards in Swiss francs to the retail price per yard in Canadian dollars – ready for Mary's inspection the following morning. And they had better be right. Mary could spot an error in mathematics, or pattern number, or quantity, with computer-like speed, and when she did, Norman was the recipient of acid criticism.

After one particularly tiring morning of sample watching in St. Gall, Switzerland, Norman and I walked a few paces behind Mary and the owner of the lace factory on our way to lunch. Contemplating spending a painful evening of order writing instead of his preferred bachelor pursuit of girl-watching, Norman was silent and thoughtful. At that moment we came upon a beggar, the only one I had ever seen in Switzerland. He was holding a tin cup toward us, selling pencils. Norman stopped, looked at the man, turned to me and remarked: "Bryant, do you know who that man is?" I confessed that I had no idea. "Well," said Norman, "he is an old Eaton's buyer. He came over here to buy laces in 1926 and never got around to writing his orders."

I have no idea whether the clock buyer for a New York Fifth-Avenue department store, responsible for one of merchandising's classic stories, had a sense of humour; but I am sure it would have helped him through one of his most trying experiences.

Prior to World War I, Black Forest clocks from Germany were in great demand throughout the United States. The store sold one particular model in large numbers at $25. Because of inflation in Germany after the war, the buyer was able to buy a huge quantity of this clock to sell at $2.98, at a nice profit.

The promotion was well advertised through newspapers and window displays, but the clocks did not sell. With thousands of dollars tied up in a warehouse full of clocks, the horrified buyer began inquiring from his salespeople as to what had gone wrong. It seemed, or so the story goes, that customers came, looked at the clocks, shook their heads, and walked away. Some were heard to mumble that it was not possible to buy a $25 clock for $2.98. "But," cried the buyer, "the clocks are identical to our $25 clock." "Customers don't believe it," was the response. With that, the buyer is reported to have whipped the clocks off sale, stored them for six months and then advertised them at "half price," $12.50. The result – a sell out!

Occasionally attempts at humour backfire. When I worked for Robert Simpson in the housewares department of The Bay in Winnipeg, the General Electric salesman was a fellow named Jackson. He was an extrovert who always bounced into the department with some wisecrack, but he was also a super salesman. My brother-in-law, Frank Wade, operated a pharmacy in Norwood, just across the Red River from Winnipeg. Jackson, who lived in Norwood, would often drop into the drug store on his way to work to chat with Frank.

Early one morning he noisily entered the store, demanding his nickels back on a number of empty bottles which had contained Canada Dry ginger ale. (This was at the time of Jack Benny's famed radio campaign.) What Jackson did not know, but soon found out, was that an armed man had taken over the store. The man had tied Frank up with wire, then thrown him on the floor of the dispensary, torn the telephone off the wall, and was searching for drugs when Jackson entered. The robber stuck a gun in Jackson's back, remarking that there would be no nickels back and no more joking. Jackson agreed. Frightened as never before in his life, he was tied up, tossed on the floor beside Frank, and told to keep quiet. He did. Soon the intruder heard police sirens in the distance and fled. Minutes passed before Frank or Jackson spoke. Eventually Jackson blurted out, "For God's sake, Wade, I can't hang around here all day. I'm supposed to be working for GE."

Jackson remembered that Frank had suggested one day not long before that he might be in the market for a washing machine for his wife, Amy. Jackson described the wonders of the GE machine so enthusiastically that Frank agreed to buy, and signed up as soon as they were untied. Jackson felt that the best part of a morning had not been wasted after all. At least thirty years later, the machine remained (functioning perfectly!) in the Wade home. I suggested that they should retain it as a monument to a super salesman.

Unfortunately, the episode had an unhappy ending. While leaving the area, the bandit realized that he was not the object of the first police pursuit. He returned to the store, not knowing that the delivery boy had reported for work and had been sent to the service station across the street to phone the police. A chase ensued, which ended in the CNR yards across the river in Winnipeg. A policeman was murdered. The robber was hanged.

*   *   *

One merchant whose sense of humour enhances the effectiveness of business discussions, is Allan Burton, Simpsons chairman and chief executive officer. He really enjoys a good belly-laugh – especially if he has told the joke. And he tells many.

Often his joke is one he has adopted from a close associate, who must sit and listen to an embellished version of his filched tale. Although he plagiarizes with abandon, his embellishments usually add enough to the story to justify the crime.

But while he is a highly-skilled raconteur, he is a lousy listener – at least to my jokes! He claims I take too long to get to the punch line. I claim it is because of his interruptions, which come so fast that it is difficult to get in a one-liner such as: "How do you make holy water? You just boil" – lengthy interruption – "the hell out of it." He must be right though, because my wife agrees with him. Sometimes he gets more laughs out of his interruptions than out of his own jokes, but he also misses some good opportunities to add stories to his own repertoire.

One story I have given up trying to complete in his presence, can now be told. That is, unless he has a direct line to the editor.

A bachelor who had made a modest fortune in the furniture business in Grand Rapids, Michigan, sold his company and took a long-delayed vacation in Europe. On his return, he bumped into a friend who implored him to tell him all about Paris as he had always planned a visit to that romantic city! The furniture man was only too glad to accommodate. He had had a marvelous time in Paris. The very first night, as he was strolling along the Champs Elysées, a beautiful young woman approached him from the opposite direction. They stopped, smiled at each other. Although one spoke no English and the other no French, that did not turn out to be much of a deterrent, and they began to walk down the long thoroughfare, arm in arm.

As they passed a sidewalk cafe, the girl indicated that she was hungry. In the cafe the young man very much wished to do the right thing – order a bottle of wine. Unable to speak to the waiter, he borrowed a pencil and drew a bottle of wine on the paper tablecloth. The waiter got the message at once. The wine must have had some effect on him, because he became quite exhilarated and began to move closer to the girl. Another bottle of wine seemed in order; the pencil was borrowed again. The second bottle resulted in somewhat closer contact with the girl. After consuming a third bottle, ordered by a pencilled drawing, the young man, daringly romantic, put his arm around the girl. But she gently pushed him away, picked up the pencil and carefully drew on the cloth a picture of a bed. "And do you know," exclaimed the traveller, "from that day to this, I have never been able to understand how she knew that I had been in the furniture business in Grand Rapids, Michigan."

This may not be a department store story, but it is at least about merchandise. Whether Allan or anyone else considers it worth retelling is unimportant to me. What is important is that finally I could finish it.

I included this section partly to show that the merchants who run department stores have made their business about as human as any commercial enterprise can be. The merchandising philosophy has been introduced hand in hand with the drollery because it never can, or should, be divorced from the human element. Perhaps those on the inside of department stores, the merchants and those who would like to be merchants, will benefit, however slightly. Perhaps those on the outside, the customers, will be enlightened. Above all, I hope both insiders and outsiders will be amused by what has been chronicled in this chapter, and by the following concluding anecdotes.

*   *   *

The dreams of architects designing department stores often turn out to be nightmares for the merchants who operate them.

The large and beautiful downtown store of the Hudson's Bay Company in Winnipeg is a case in point. The designers may have consulted with the merchants who were to run the store, but they couldn't possibly have discussed vertical transportation!

Although the store opened in 1926, escalators were virtually ignored. To carry customers to upper floors, two huge banks of elevators were located facing each other, slightly to the rear of centre in the square building. The elevators were arranged in concave configurations so that the opening between them was elliptical in shape, like a football with the points cut off. The ends of the elevator lobby were about twenty feet wide. At the centre of the two banks, the distance was about forty feet.

Each bank contained six elevators, so that the length of the egg-shaped area was about sixty feet in all.

From the day the store opened, the elevator lobby was a headache for store management. The only other vertical transportation in the entire store consisted of two narrow, wooden escalators on the outside of the elevator banks. As these travelled only to the second floor and the basement, and carried only one person per step, they were virtually useless.

The consequences of this layout was that every customer wishing to visit any floor other than the main one, congregated in the elevator lobby. It was so restricted in size and shape that even small crowds caused utter confusion. A starter was ineffective, as customers usually prevented a clear view of the elevator doors. Customers ran back and forth to catch elevators, only to have doors close as they reached them. Many became convinced that all the elevators on one side only went up and those on the other side only went down, an idea encouraged by some management trainees who, despite the scarcity of jobs, were not above having a little joke at the customers' expense.

A frustrated Mr. Gilbert, merchandise manager of the store, directed me, as his research assistant, to make a study of the problem and come up with a solution. The study did not take long, and the solution did not require much imagination. In fact, it was rather obvious: take one bank of elevators out and replace it with wide, high-speed escalators.

When I proposed this course of action to Mr. Gilbert, he invited me to leave his office, suggesting that I had little conception of construction costs and little knowledge of how the increased capital expenditure would make it even more difficult to make a profit. I retreated, deflated. But, after the war, when money became more plentiful, this is precisely how The Bay solved its vertical transportation problem.

In the meantime, the perplexing situation remained, and more thought was devoted to it. Eventually, someone came up with the idea that the centre area should be turned into a shop to sell merchandise. The rationale was that customers would no longer be able to rush back and forth between elevator banks, and they could use that time to buy things rather than venting their frustrations with unkind thoughts and ugly words about the stupid store managers.

The area was entitled the "New Things Shop." Mr. Gilbert, perhaps as a punishment for my failure to suggest something more practical than a vast construction project, added the supervision of the shop to my many other duties.

The plan was to collect new items from various departments in the store and display them for short periods so that a constant flow of new, fresh merchandise was presented. Moreover, when store executives visited exotic places, they minimized their personal expenses by purchasing great quantities of merchandise, usually unsalable, for the shop.

In my short career as supervisor, only one lot of such merchandise arrived that evoked the slightest interest on the part of customers. On a Mexican holiday, someone had purchased an assortment of glassware, basketware, and serapes that began to sell as soon as it was placed on display.

Whenever I had occasion to pass the "New Things Shop," I made a quick check to make sure that the displays were in order and that obvious things were not being overlooked. I was so elated at the sales of the Mexican merchandise, as this degree of customer reaction was unusual, that the thought ran through my mind that perhaps it was being stolen rather than sold!

When any item sells well (as the Mexican merchandise did), a merchant's immediate reaction is, "How soon can I get more?" I wanted to demonstrate to everyone in the store that I was learning the merchandising game quickly. I directed the girl in charge of the shop to obtain new supplies from the stockroom immediately. About a half hour later I returned to find, to my great annoyance, that nothing had happened. The girl explained that she had been unable to locate the stock boy but would take care of it at once.

When, an hour later, still nothing had happened, I demanded to know where that particular merchandise was being stored. I'd get the damned stuff myself!

Unused fitting rooms on the third floor had been assigned to the Mexican goods, I was told, and I rushed off to that part of the store with rather imprecise directions. I hurried down a long hall with fitting rooms on either side and barged into the one I assumed to be the stockroom. There, quite naked, was a girl about to try on a foundation garment. Backing out in utter confusion and embarrassment, I had barely enough time to note that she had a rather pleasing figure, albeit one which required correction in spots.

Somehow I had lost my appetite for haste and slowly returned to my own desk on the perimeter of a large general office area across an aisle from my boss' office. There were many desks in the larger area, occupied by men and women doing various accounting tasks which, unlike my job, kept them tied down all day. I suddenly became aware of laughter around and about. The girl in the fitting room was now stationed a few desks away from mine, informing her associates that the mystery of my long absences from my desk had been solved: according to her, I was spending my time peeking into fitting rooms!

*   *   *

My two last flings at merchandising did not take place in any department store. In retrospect, these events seem very funny to me but while they were taking place, I had to remind myself continually that a good merchant must maintain his sense of humour, especially when things go wrong.

The first of these ventures was a garage sale. My retirement involved moving to an apartment in Toronto for the summers and to a house in Florida for the winters. As we prepared for the moving company, it became obvious to me that such a sale was the only practicable way to rid ourselves of the odds and ends which collect over many years in a seventeen-room house.

My wife objected. In the first place, she did not quite understand garage sales. About a year earlier, when a friend who had sold his house talked about having a garage sale, she wondered aloud why he had not sold his garage along with the house. Also, in her view, any such sale would be most inappropriate in our section of Outremont, considered (by those who live there) to be the poshest suburb on the Island of Montreal. Eventually, however, I was able to persuade my wife if not to participate, at least to go along with the project since we were leaving the area, and I set out to stage the best garage sale ever.

I hardly needed to remind myself of the various elements required to produce a successful promotion. Value – the right quality and style at the right price – is the first and most important merchandising factor. The advertising copy must be easy to read and crystal clear. The merchandise must be arranged for the convenience of customers. The signs on the merchandise must be prominent, show the prices plainly, and provide all pertinent information. And, the sale must be held at just the right time – the right day of the week, the right day of the month.

Timing! This factor is nearly as important as the merchandise itself, an axiom I had been preaching to my protégés in the department store business from the time I became hooked on the merchandising game.

The incident that had convinced me to become a retailer, rather than a chemist for which profession I had studied, occurred when I was a salesman responsible for stock control of small electrical appliances at The Bay in Winnipeg. To the aspiring young merchants who I hope will read this book, the story should, at the least, bear repeating.

Electric irons with thermostatic heat-control knobs had recently been placed on the market. Three well-known makes – General Electric, Westinghouse, and Universal – were all priced identically at $7.50. This was an astronomical price, compared to the $2.95 tag on irons without heat controls and to promotional irons which sold for as little as $1.00. Moreover, any retailer who dared to sell heat-controlled irons for less than $7.50, the manufacturer's set price, was at once cut off from all supplies of that maker's products. Price fixing was a way of life in those days.

Under the circumstances, little imagination was required to conclude that a good heat-controlled iron priced at about $4.95 would be in great demand. Accordingly, when a representative of Dominion Electric Company, a small Winnipeg wholesaler, informed me that he had available five hundred such irons, I rushed to Robert Simpson, the department manager, and implored him to buy them. On the strength of my assurances that they would sell like hotcakes, he did.

The plan was to promote the irons with such an effective advertisement that the entire five hundred would be disposed of in one day. That quantity was the equivalent of, perhaps, ten thousand today.

My idea would be a merchandising scoop, to say the least. I suggested, almost insisted in fact, that the ad be run in Tuesday evening's papers.

"Why?" asked Mr. Simpson, the department manager.

"Because," I explained, "Tuesday is ironing day, except when it rains on Monday. Tuesday is the day when housewives all over town find out that their irons have gone on the blink. Every Tuesday, I am continually called to the telephone by harrassed women whose irons are in need of repairs. If the ad appears Tuesday night, these women will be explaining their iron problems to their husbands about the time the husbands are reading our advertisement. Or the husbands may be tripping over laundry baskets filled with unironed clothes as their wives are reading our ad aloud. Either way, we are in business."

I reached the store shortly after 7:00 a.m. on the Wednesday after the advertisement appeared, although my early arrival was quite unnecessary. All five hundred irons had been placed on display the evening before. Those out of cartons had been polished until the chrome finish showed signs of wear. There were huge signs in the elevator lobby showing the way to the point of sale and appropriate signs on the sides of cartons containing irons. I merely had to wait until the store opened, in about two hours, I thought. The wait was painful, but at long last the first elevator stopped at our floor. I fully expected it to be carrying a swarm of iron customers. It was empty! Another elevator. Also empty. A feeling began to develop in the pit of my stomach that I was to come to recognize very well in the years ahead. Then, about fifteen minutes after the store opened, one man turned up to inspect the advertised irons. I presume he arrived by elevator, but by this time I could not bear to look in that direction. He bought one. A few phone calls came in, and a few more customers appeared. Soon they did arrive in the droves I had expected at store opening. By 11:00 a.m. the entire stock of five hundred irons had been sold, and I was hooked on retailing as a career and advertising-timing as a precept.

After that, to maximize advertising results, I implored advertising people and merchants to make sure they knew everything about the day selected for a promotion. Will there be a teachers' convention the day of the sale? Teachers' convention means a school holiday. School holiday means promote teen fashions and children's wear. Does Hallowe'en fall on a night on which the store will be open? If so, do not promote furniture and the like. Parents stay home on Hallowe'en so money spent on advertising is wasted. The same would be true if sporting goods were to be advertised on the night of a Stanley Cup play-off game, because most sportsmen would be watching television. No detail, I always insisted, is too small to consider.

And so, to follow one of my fundamental promotional rules, our garage sale had to be held at just the right time. I chose October 6, 1973.

The big day arrived. Like the iron sale, first "crowds" were disappointing. In fact, very few customers were present at "store opening," and my clever arrangement of merchandise, by departments, was hardly necessary for the limited number of sales.

I had used what I presumed were clever promotional techniques, especially in the signs placed on the various items and sections. For example, a sign reading "Electrical Junk, Everything in Box $3" was placed on a carton containing a few extension cords, plug caps, and odds and ends of wire.

One customer remarked to Miss Rivet, my secretary, whose help I had enlisted when my wife disdained participation, that the carton surely contained a bunch of junk. He wished to buy only a few of the better pieces and a price of two dollars was agreed upon. The sign was left on the carton and, sure enough, a short time later another customer bought the rest of the box for three dollars.

But my garage sale was best described by Julian Benbow, Simpsons general sales promotion manager, at a later gathering of my associates. He related to the group, with unnecessary relish I thought, that it had been a sale that could not fail. The merchandise was right; it came from my own home; I had bought it myself. The advertising was right; I had written the copy and selected the media myself. The displays were right; I had prepared them myself. The signs were right; I had lettered them myself. And the timing – it certainly was right; I had personally selected the date.

But wait, Julian had said, Outremont has a large Jewish population. Further, the community is adjacent to the suburb with the greatest concentration of Jewish families on the Island of Montreal. Perhaps half my prospective garage-sale customers would be Jewish. But then, how was I to know that October 6, 1973, would be Yom Kippur?

As things turned out, I was to have one more chance.

When we moved from our home in Outremont the household furniture was divided. Some was shipped to Florida, and four large containers were placed in storage for use in a Toronto apartment which we planned to select at a later date.

We spent the winter in Florida, delaying our return north with each weather report. By the time we reached Toronto in June, we realized that it made little sense to rent an apartment on a yearly basis for only three or four months actual use.

As a result, the containers would have to be retrieved from storage and the contents sorted once again and disposed of as circumstances dictated. An area the size of two or three rooms would be required. Surprisingly, the storage company had no such facility. Attempts to rent a church hall or a school basement failed.

Then, one evening, while we were out for a stroll, my wife and I noticed an empty store. The obvious answer! We located one on North Avenue Road in Toronto, which the owner, a Mrs. Angelini, agreed to rent for two weeks. The store had previously been leased by an antique dealer who had gone bankrupt, but who had left his signs painted on the windows. (It now houses Angelini's Dining Room, about the best place in Toronto for Italian food.)

As we unpacked the containers and arranged furniture, clothing, household effects, and a number of antiques around the store, passers-by naturally assumed that a new antique shop was being set up. We were kept busy explaining that, while some things would be for sale later on, our first task was deciding what should be done with each item.

The decisions made, we invited young friends of our two married sons to have the first selection of the items which were to be sold. Then we ran advertisements in the classified columns of the daily newspapers.

The response could hardly be described as overwhelming, but after a few days most of the good items were sold. Except for the antiques, that is. Despite the signs on the windows, the antiques did not move at all. To be sure, many people came into the store looking for antiques, but they usually had specific items in mind, like cranberry-glass wine glasses or old paper weights. Moreover, the antiques we were prepared to sell were obviously too highly priced.

Soon, modern department store practices were thrown overboard, and haggling was the manner in which all sales were completed. People we took a liking to, mostly young married couples, got the bargains. Those who rubbed us the wrong way paid, One woman annoyed me by offering fifteen dollars for a set of lead-crystal tumblers when I asked for thirty. I made her pay forty.

Our store was open for just two weeks. As the stock of furniture, home furnishings, and other desirable items diminished, so did the flow of customers. We did develop, nevertheless, a sort of clientele. Some of these regular customers came back as many as two or three times a day to see if a desired item was still available and if its price had been reduced.

One of these was a little, old, misshapen woman who, we concluded, must have been running a second-hand store nearby. She picked up, carefully fingered, and replaced every piece of clothing, bits and pieces of china, dolls, and other toys.

After endless haggling she occasionally made a purchase at a price under one dollar. She always explained that she was old and poor. She was obviously old, but we doubted that she was poor.

Frequently, during the final days of the operation, when I was alone in the store sitting on a borrowed director's chair and reading a book I had salvaged from a carton on its way to a senior citizens home, the little old lady or one of the other regulars dropped in. By this time, only a pathetic group of china, glassware, and housewares remained. Whenever one of these customers entered the store, I put down my book and started negotiations.

"What are you asking for this cream and sugar set?"

"Two dollars."

"I'll give you a dollar."

"No, a dollar and a half."

And so it went. Incredibly, it was not until later, while describing the event to a friend, that I saw the humour in the situation. There I was, a man who, less than a year earlier, had occupied a huge office and managed a large department store organization, bargaining with a second-hand dealer in an attempt to extract an extra fifty cents from her for a bit of china or glassware which was perhaps only worth a quarter in the first place.

The friend reminded me of a joke I used to tell whenever I or one of my associates would become overly impressed by a position or title. The story went something like this – always in the first person!

When I was appointed a vice-president, I came home and announced to the family that I was now a vice-president and that I would appreciate it if they would show me a little more respect than they had in the past. Things didn't change much, however, so I felt compelled to remind them again, and again, of my now exalted title and position. One day my wife, Bea, said: "Oh, knock it off. Vice-presidents are a dime a dozen. Why I was in the Dominion Store the other day and the manager told me they even had a vice-president of prunes." "That's ridiculous," I replied, but I made a mental note to check up on her statement – just in case. The following morning I phoned the head office of Dominion Stores and asked to speak to the vice-president of prunes. The reply was both instantaneous and unforgettable: "Packaged or unpackaged?"

On the final afternoon, my wife, feeling depressed from sadly sifting through portfolios of the artwork of our daughter who had died some three years earlier as a result of a car accident, went to visit a friend, and I was sitting alone with my own sad thoughts, waiting for the Salvation Army truck to pick up a large carton of linens and blankets. On top of the carton lay an old cloche-style hat that had somehow escaped being sent with my wife's old dresses to the nearly new shop of a women's charitable organization.

The door opened for yet another visit from the little old second-hand-store lady. She wandered about the place in silence until she spotted the hat. She picked it up, felt it thoroughly, looked inside at the labels and lining, and then carefully placed it on her head. She approached a mirror on the wall of the store and appraised herself skeptically.

"How much do you want for it?" she inquired.

"Two dollars," I replied. Completely disregarding my knowledge of merchandise values, I had started all bidding at two dollars in those final few days.

Fifty cents was her counter offer.

I then seized upon the opportunity to realize a merchandising ambition I had harboured for many years but had never quite been able to achieve. Before I retired, when I visited the selling floors, I occasionally encountered markdown racks of shopworn, dirty, and out-of-fashion dresses. To emphasize to our merchants the vital merchandising principle of marking down fashion merchandise the very second sales begin to slow, I reminded them that an old fashion was as perishable as an old banana and about as appealing to our customers. I further suggested, jokingly I presume, because as far as I know the suggestion was never followed, "Would it not be a lot better if you were to place on top of this markdown rack a large sign reading 'TAKE ONE!' "

"Fifty cents?" my customer asked again.

"No," I said, "take it."

The second-hand lady walked out wearing the hat, the Salvation Army truck arrived, and I closed the store.